A WHO HQ GRAPH

Who Was Ac
the Salem Witch Trials?

TITUBA

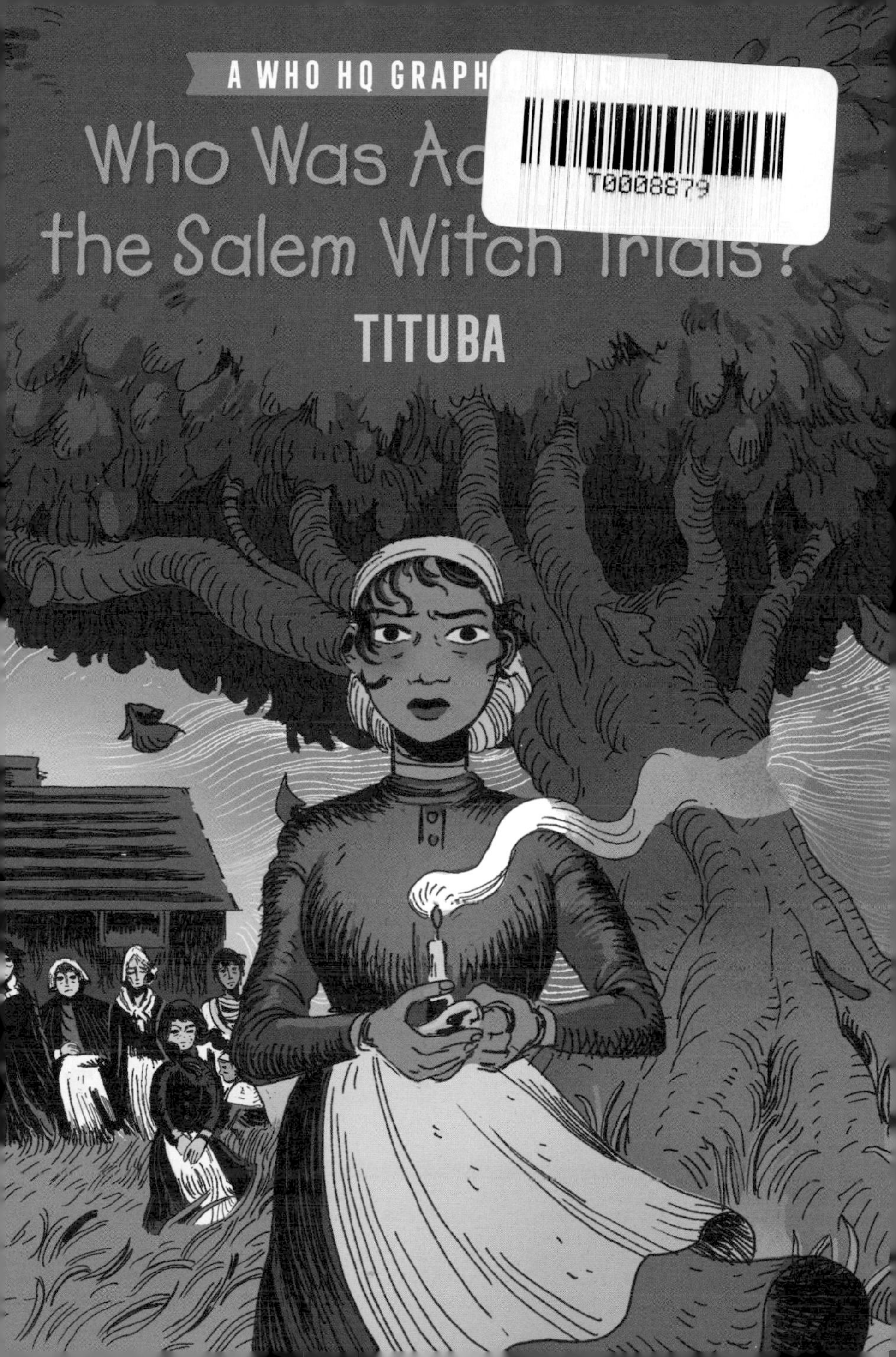

To Erin & Katie, my coven—IF

Thank you to my mom, my dad, my sister, and my five cats
for always being loving, supportive, and helping me become
the artist I am today (mostly the cats though)—RM

PENGUIN WORKSHOP
An imprint of Penguin Random House LLC, New York

First published in the United States of America by Penguin Workshop,
an imprint of Penguin Random House LLC, New York, 2023

Visit us online at penguinrandomhouse.com.

Library of Congress Cataloging-in-Publication Data is available.

Manufactured in China

ISBN 9780593224687 (pbk)   10 9 8 7 6 5 4 3 2 1 HH
ISBN 9780593224694 (hc)   10 9 8 7 6 5 4 3 2 1 HH

Lettering by Comicraft
Design by Jay Emmanuel

This is a work of nonfiction. All of the events that unfold in the narrative
are rooted in historical fact. Some dialogue and characters have been fictionalized
in order to illustrate or teach a historical point.

The publisher does not have any control over and does not assume any
responsibility for author or third-party websites or their content.

For more information about your favorite historical figures, places, and events,
please visit whohq.com.

A WHO HQ GRAPHIC NOVEL

Who Was Accused in the Salem Witch Trials?

TITUBA

by Insha Fitzpatrick
illustrated by Rowan MacColl

Penguin Workshop

Introduction

In the cold winter morning light of 1691, Tituba woke up and began her day as she always had: with a list of daily chores. She and her husband, John Indian, served the home of Reverend Samuel Parris and his wife, Elizabeth. Reverend Parris was a minister of the Puritan religion, a Christian movement practiced by the English people who colonized much of New England at the time, including Massachusetts Bay, Rhode Island, and Connecticut.

Tituba was far from home—she is believed to have been born in an Arawak tribe village in Venezuela in 1674 and was later kidnapped and taken to Barbados where she was enslaved and sold to Reverend Parris. He then moved Tituba and his family—which included his children Elizabeth "Betty" Parris, Thomas Parris, Susannah Parris, and their cousin Abigail Williams—to Salem Village, a wealthy Puritan community in the Massachusetts Bay colony.

Tituba's duties included nearly all the housework: laundry, getting water from the wells, scrubbing floors, and being a caretaker to the children. In fact, Tituba had a young daughter, too—a three-year-old girl named Violet. On this particular morning, she began by filling up a large bucket with boiling water to start the seasonal laundry but felt a tug at the end of her dress. It was Betty and Abigail—they wanted to hear more stories of Tituba's life before her arrival to New England.

As the winter progressed, more children came to hear Tituba's stories. She told them stories not only of her life, but of her culture. One night, after the visiting girls went home from another evening of listening to Tituba's stories, Betty and Abigail lay wide awake in their beds. Abigail wanted to play a fortune-telling game that could help her and Betty find out who their future husbands would be—a practice the Puritans called "Venus glass." All they had to do was crack an egg white inside a jar and see what the fortune told them. It's unknown where Abigail got the spark of imagination to play this magic game. She may have been curious because these practices were forbidden by her parents and the Puritan religion, or maybe because she had heard about it from someone else.

Naturally curious, Betty also agreed to go along with Abigail's plan. They grabbed a candle and made their way to the kitchen, sneaking past Tituba, who was also up late finishing her chores.

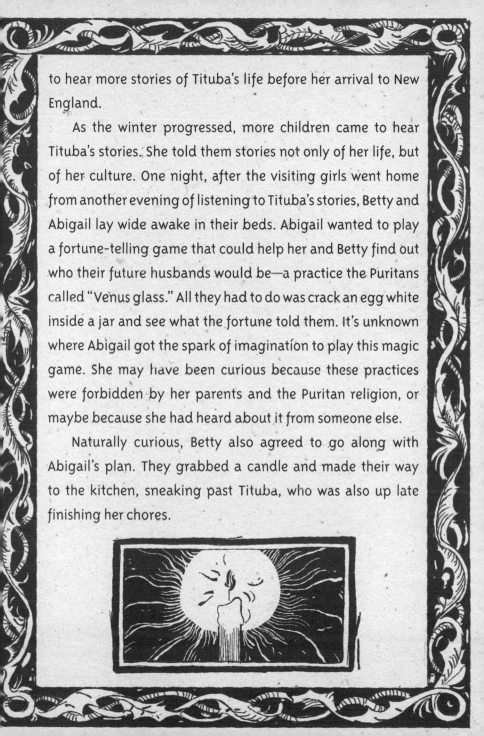

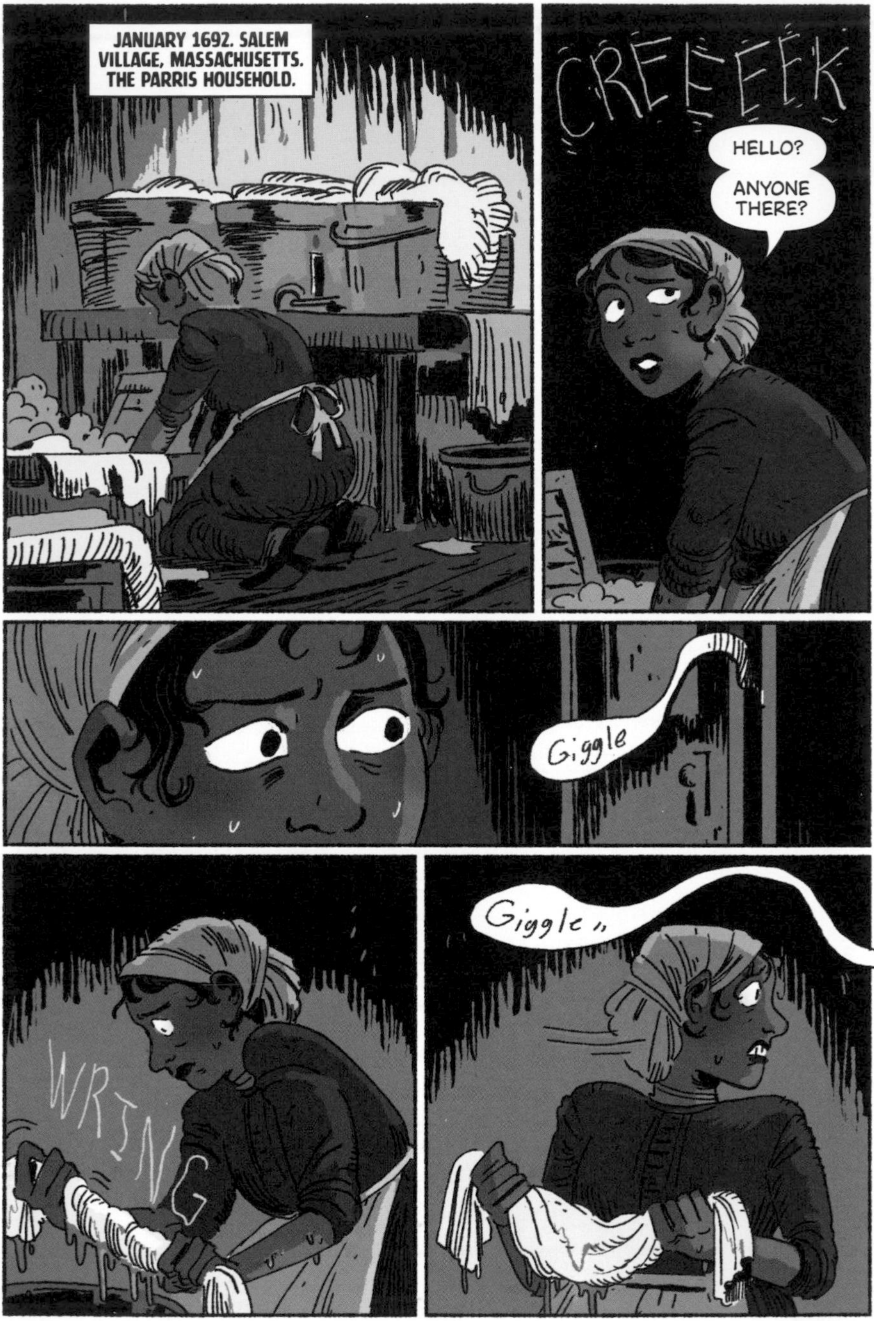
JANUARY 1692. SALEM VILLAGE, MASSACHUSETTS. THE PARRIS HOUSEHOLD.
CREEEEK
HELLO?
ANYONE THERE?
Giggle
Giggle ,,
WRING

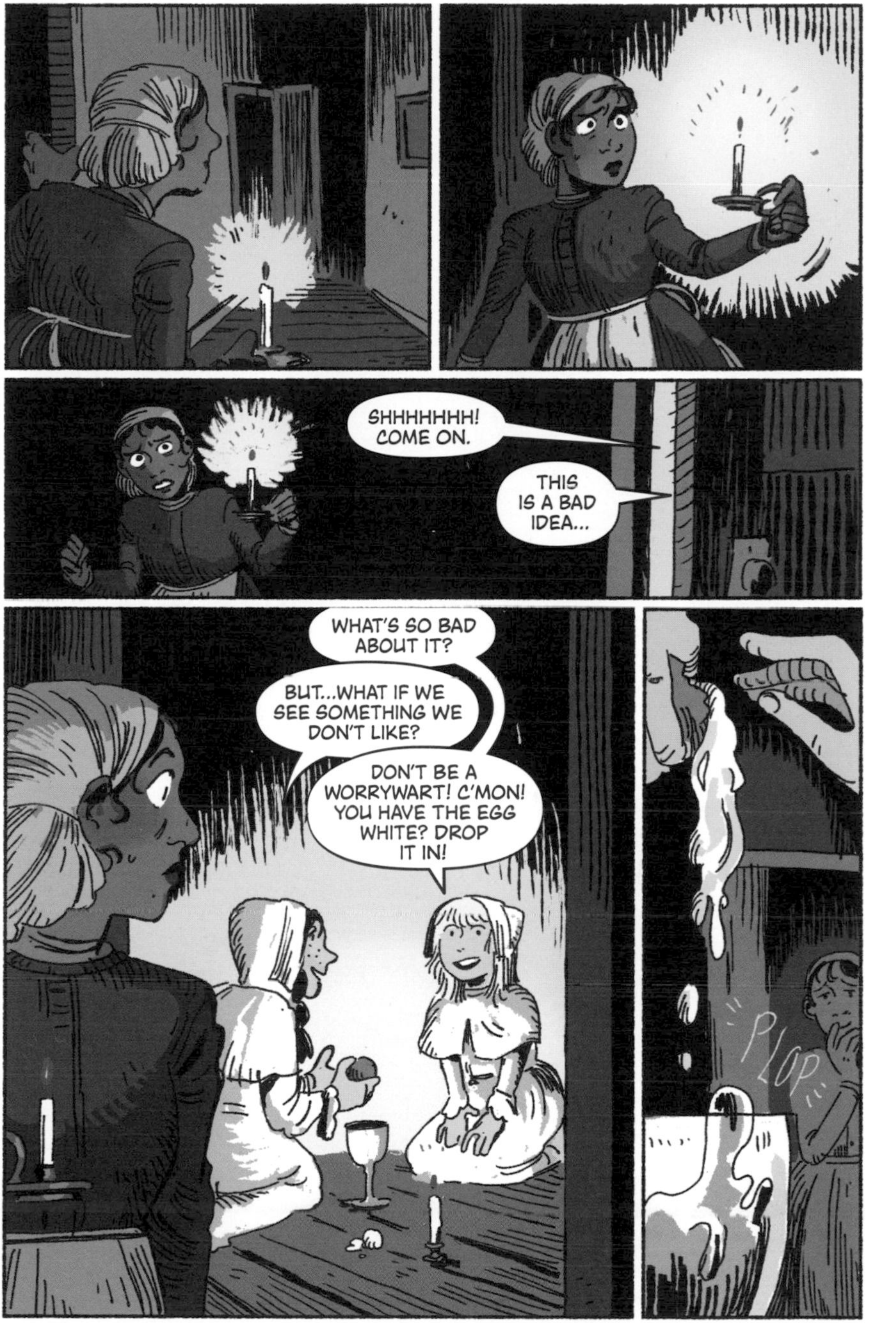
SHHHHHHH! COME ON.
THIS IS A BAD IDEA...
WHAT'S SO BAD ABOUT IT?
BUT...WHAT IF WE SEE SOMETHING WE DON'T LIKE?
DON'T BE A WORRYWART! C'MON! YOU HAVE THE EGG WHITE? DROP IT IN!
PLOP

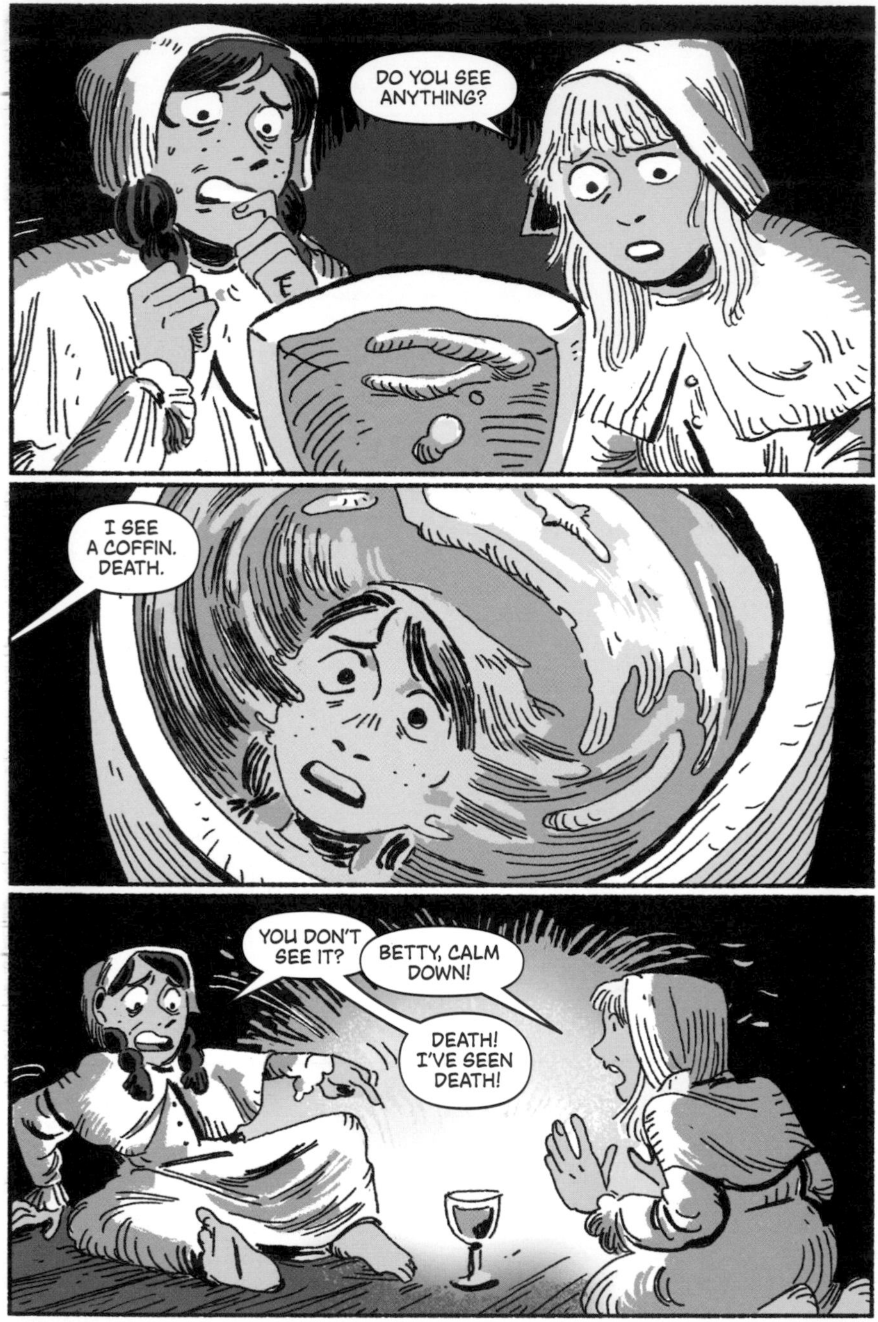
DO YOU SEE ANYTHING?
I SEE A COFFIN. DEATH.
YOU DON'T SEE IT?
BETTY, CALM DOWN!
DEATH! I'VE SEEN DEATH!

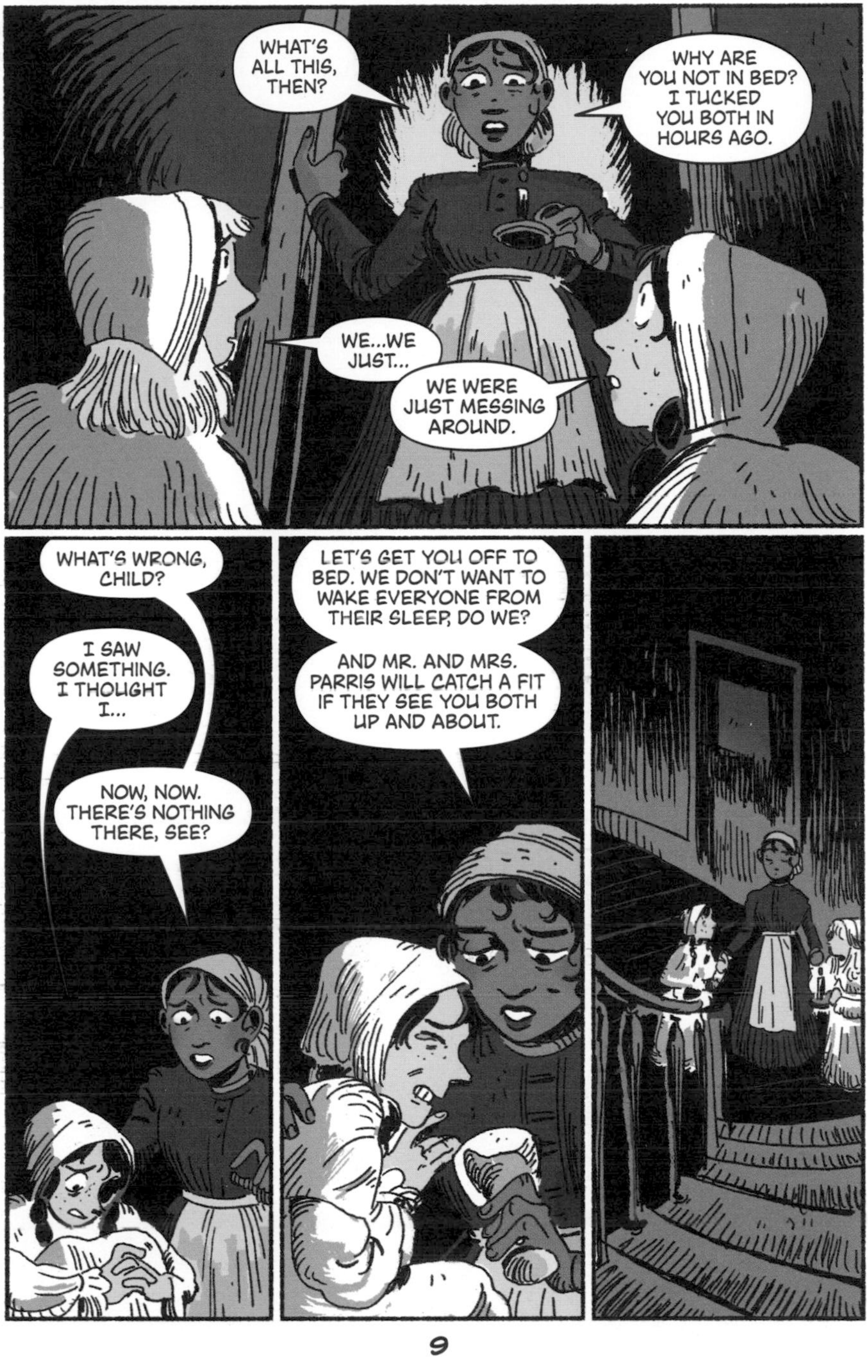
WHAT'S ALL THIS, THEN?
WHY ARE YOU NOT IN BED? I TUCKED YOU BOTH IN HOURS AGO.
WE...WE JUST...
WE WERE JUST MESSING AROUND.
WHAT'S WRONG, CHILD?
I SAW SOMETHING. I THOUGHT I...
NOW, NOW. THERE'S NOTHING THERE, SEE?
LET'S GET YOU OFF TO BED. WE DON'T WANT TO WAKE EVERYONE FROM THEIR SLEEP, DO WE?
AND MR. AND MRS. PARRIS WILL CATCH A FIT IF THEY SEE YOU BOTH UP AND ABOUT.

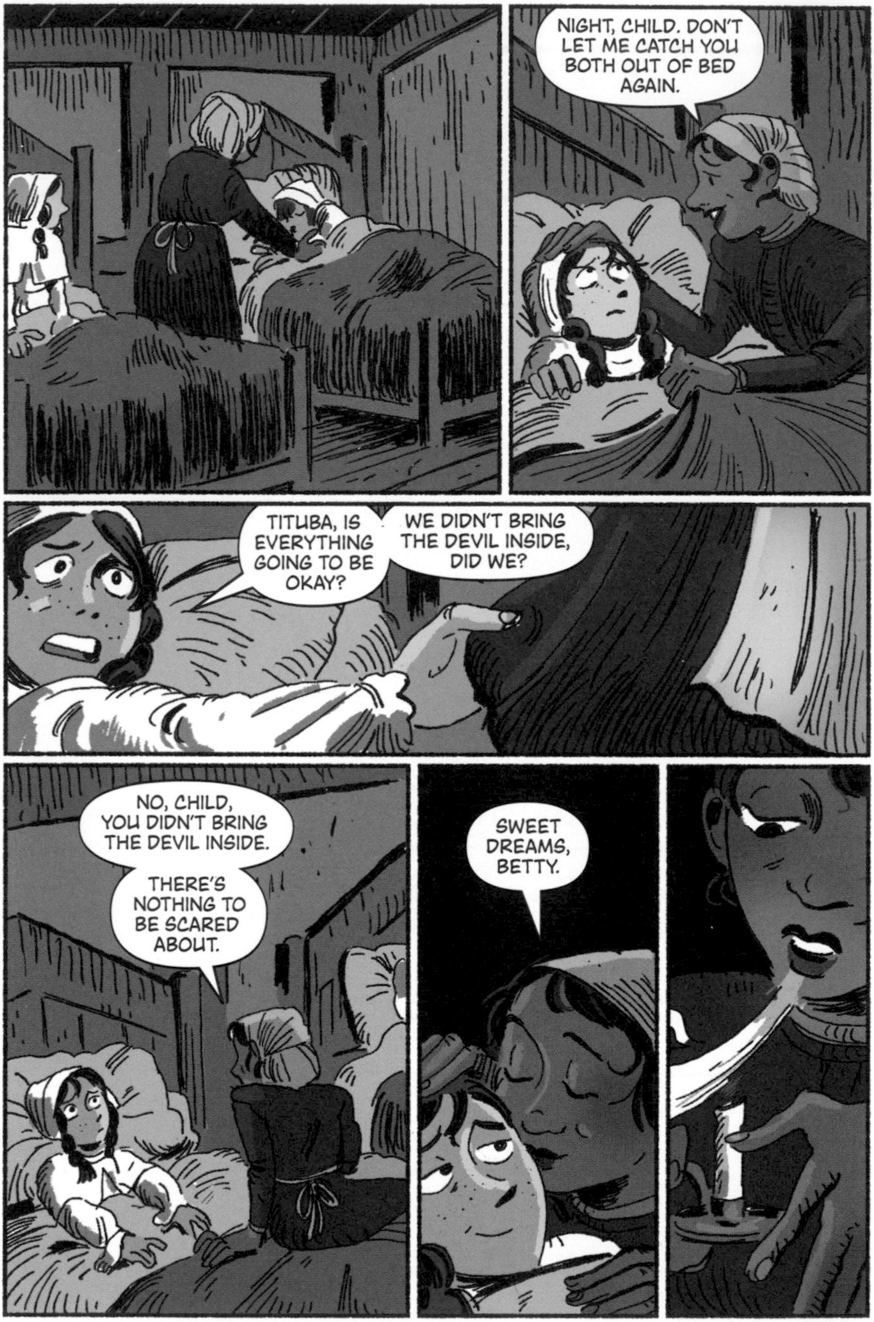
NIGHT, CHILD. DON'T LET ME CATCH YOU BOTH OUT OF BED AGAIN.
TITUBA, IS EVERYTHING GOING TO BE OKAY?
WE DIDN'T BRING THE DEVIL INSIDE, DID WE?
NO, CHILD, YOU DIDN'T BRING THE DEVIL INSIDE.
THERE'S NOTHING TO BE SCARED ABOUT.
SWEET DREAMS, BETTY.

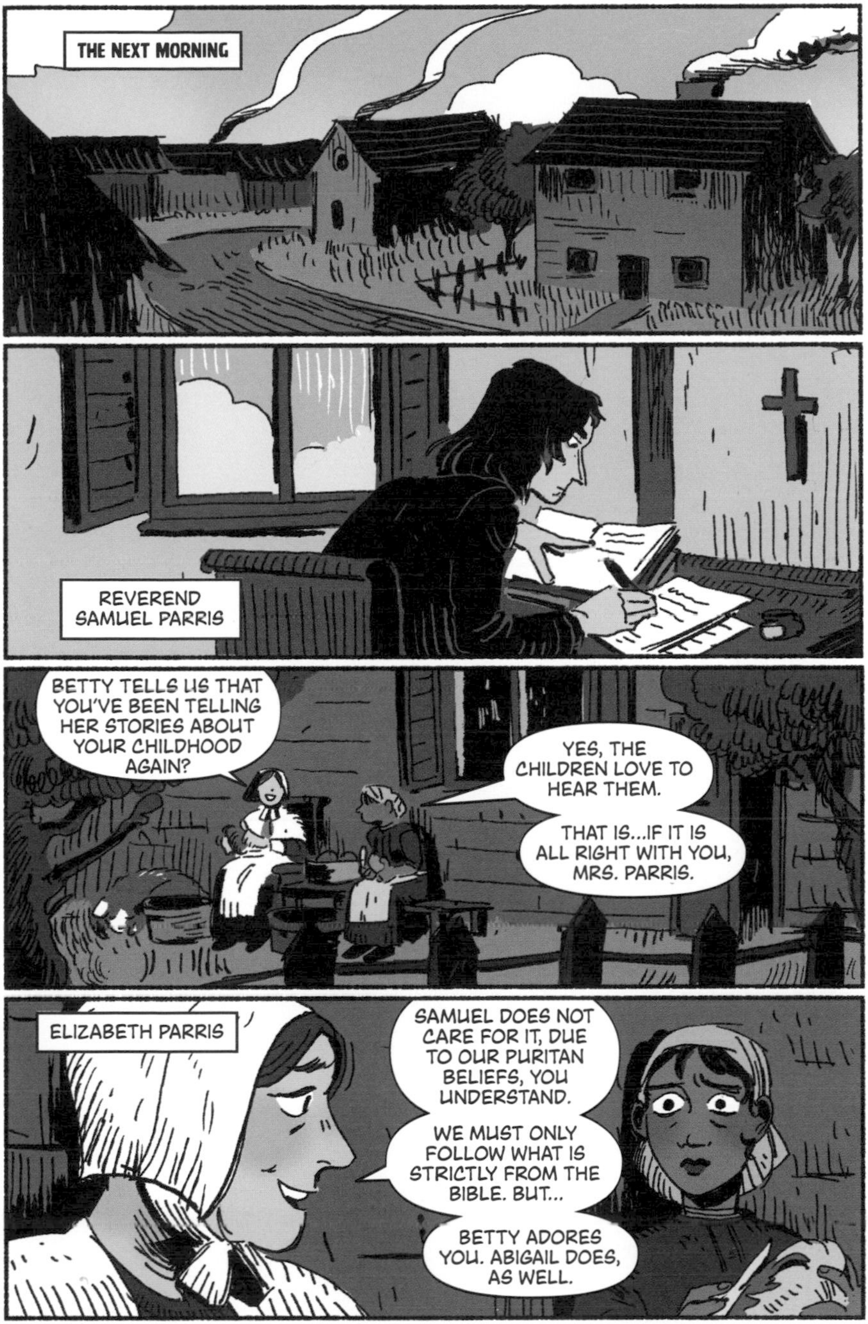
THE NEXT MORNING
REVEREND SAMUEL PARRIS
BETTY TELLS US THAT YOU'VE BEEN TELLING HER STORIES ABOUT YOUR CHILDHOOD AGAIN?
YES, THE CHILDREN LOVE TO HEAR THEM.
THAT IS...IF IT IS ALL RIGHT WITH YOU, MRS. PARRIS.
ELIZABETH PARRIS
SAMUEL DOES NOT CARE FOR IT, DUE TO OUR PURITAN BELIEFS, YOU UNDERSTAND.
WE MUST ONLY FOLLOW WHAT IS STRICTLY FROM THE BIBLE. BUT...
BETTY ADORES YOU. ABIGAIL DOES, AS WELL.

Puritans

In the 1500s, the Church of England had broken away from the Roman Catholic Church during a movement called the Protestant Reformation. But even after the separation, there was a group of people that still believed that the Church of England was far too similar to the Catholic Church. This group was called the Puritans.

Puritans wanted to strictly live by the rules of the Bible and eliminate any ceremonies or practices that strayed away from that belief.

Members of the Puritan movement believed in hard work and simplicity. They never wore fancy clothes and weren't allowed to take part in practices that they felt were "sinful," like playing games or dancing. They believed that many good things that happened were caused by God, but the bad things were caused by the Devil. Many Puritans felt that children and women were most easily influenced by the Devil, particularly if they partook in any activity outside of the Puritan religion.

In 1620, a group of Puritan separatists left England to seek religious freedom and practice their faith in North America. Many of them settled in Plymouth Colony, which is now known as Massachusetts.

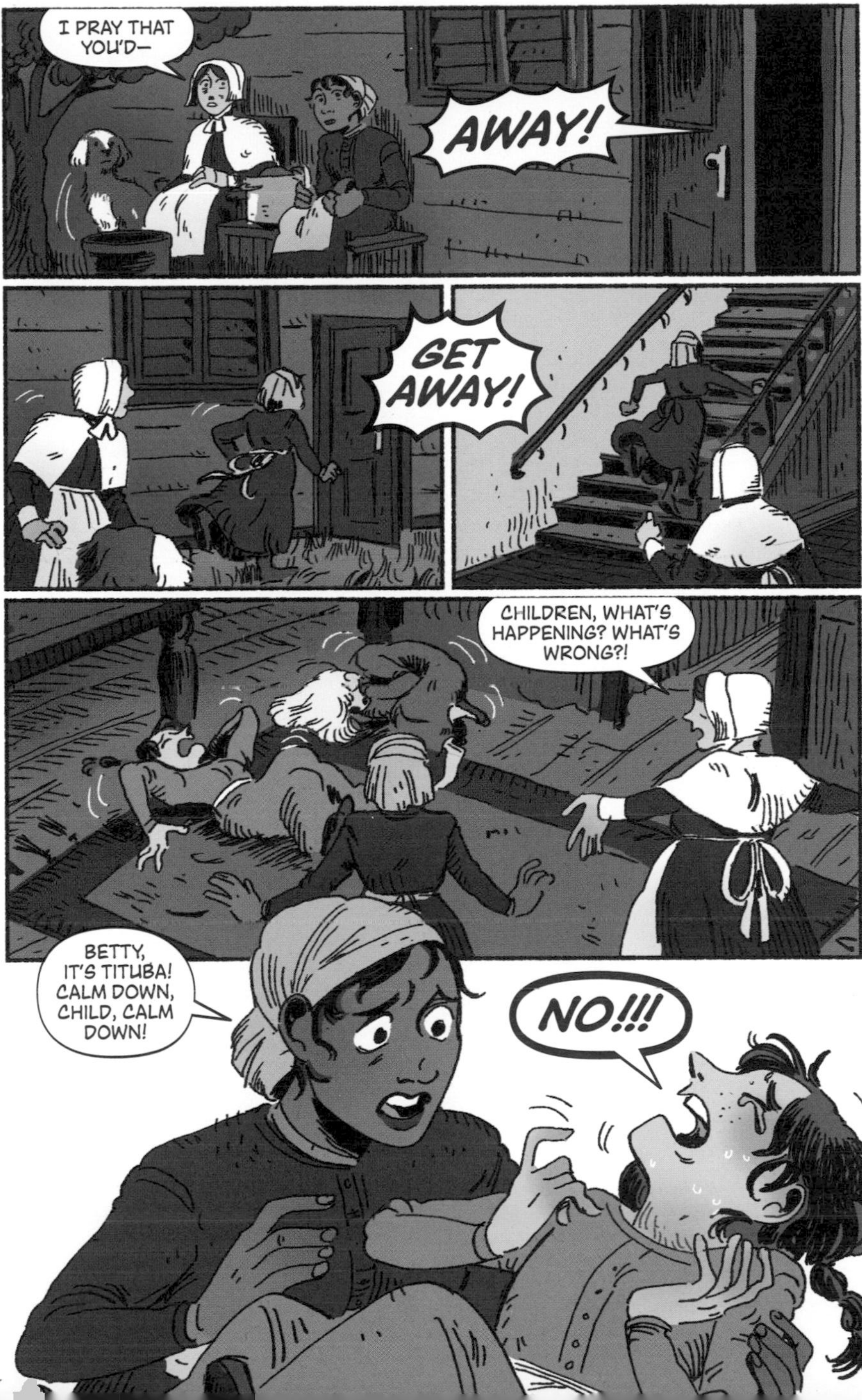
I PRAY THAT YOU'D—
AWAY!
GET AWAY!
CHILDREN, WHAT'S HAPPENING? WHAT'S WRONG?!
BETTY, IT'S TITUBA! CALM DOWN, CHILD, CALM DOWN!
NO!!!

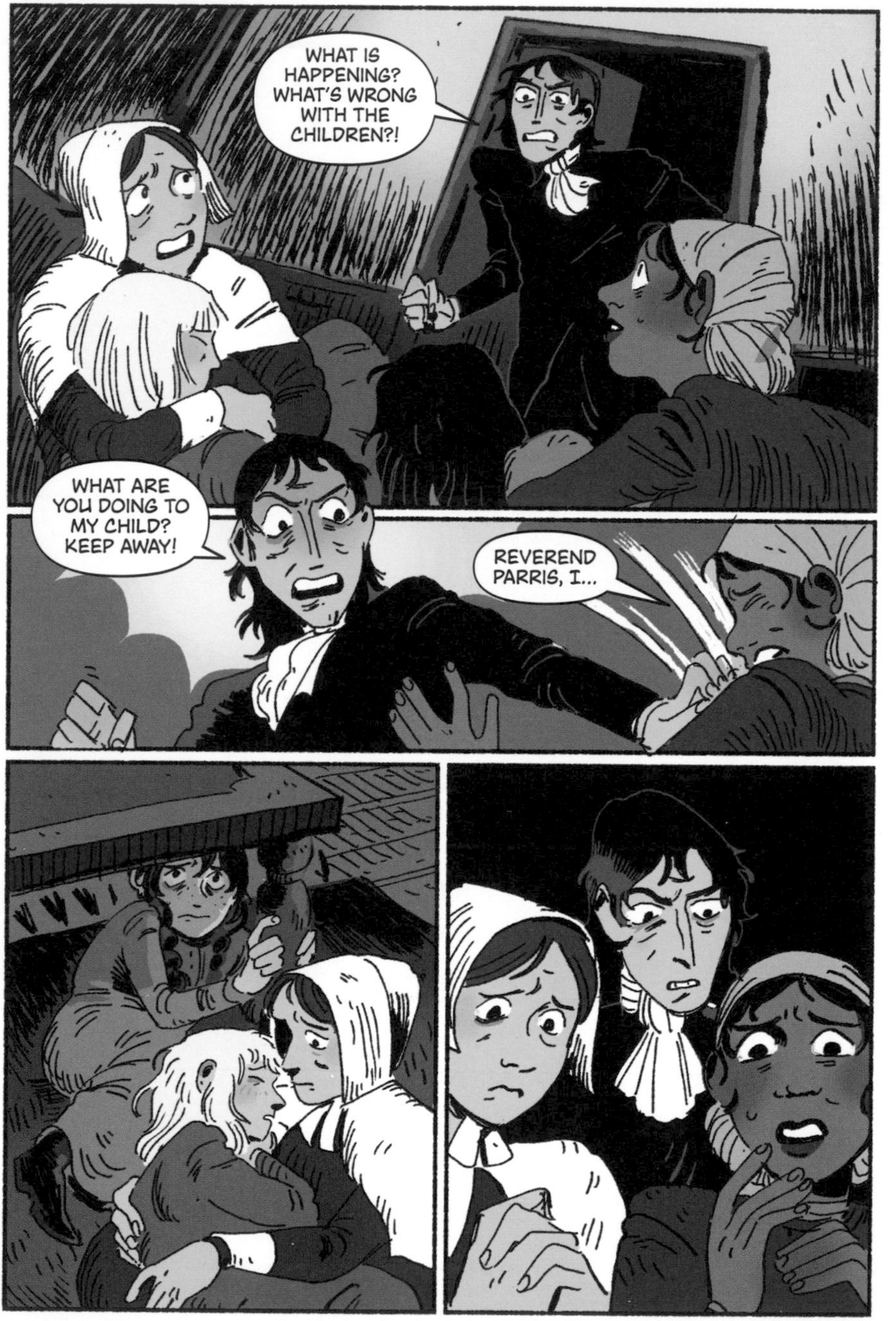
WHAT IS HAPPENING? WHAT'S WRONG WITH THE CHILDREN?!
WHAT ARE YOU DOING TO MY CHILD? KEEP AWAY!
REVEREND PARRIS, I...

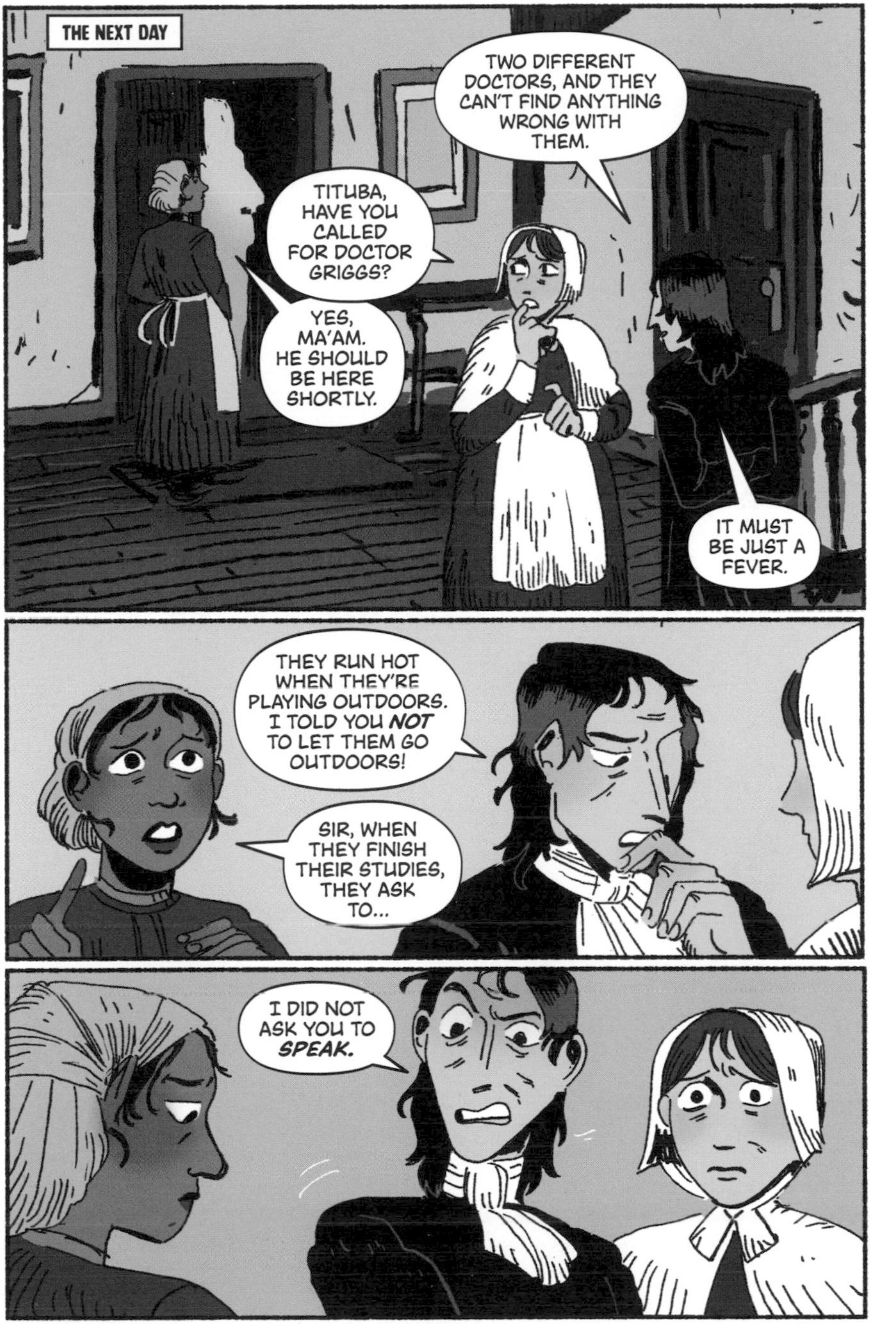
THE NEXT DAY
TWO DIFFERENT DOCTORS, AND THEY CAN'T FIND ANYTHING WRONG WITH THEM.
TITUBA, HAVE YOU CALLED FOR DOCTOR GRIGGS?
YES, MA'AM. HE SHOULD BE HERE SHORTLY.
IT MUST BE JUST A FEVER.
THEY RUN HOT WHEN THEY'RE PLAYING OUTDOORS. I TOLD YOU NOT TO LET THEM GO OUTDOORS!
SIR, WHEN THEY FINISH THEIR STUDIES, THEY ASK TO...
I DID NOT ASK YOU TO SPEAK.

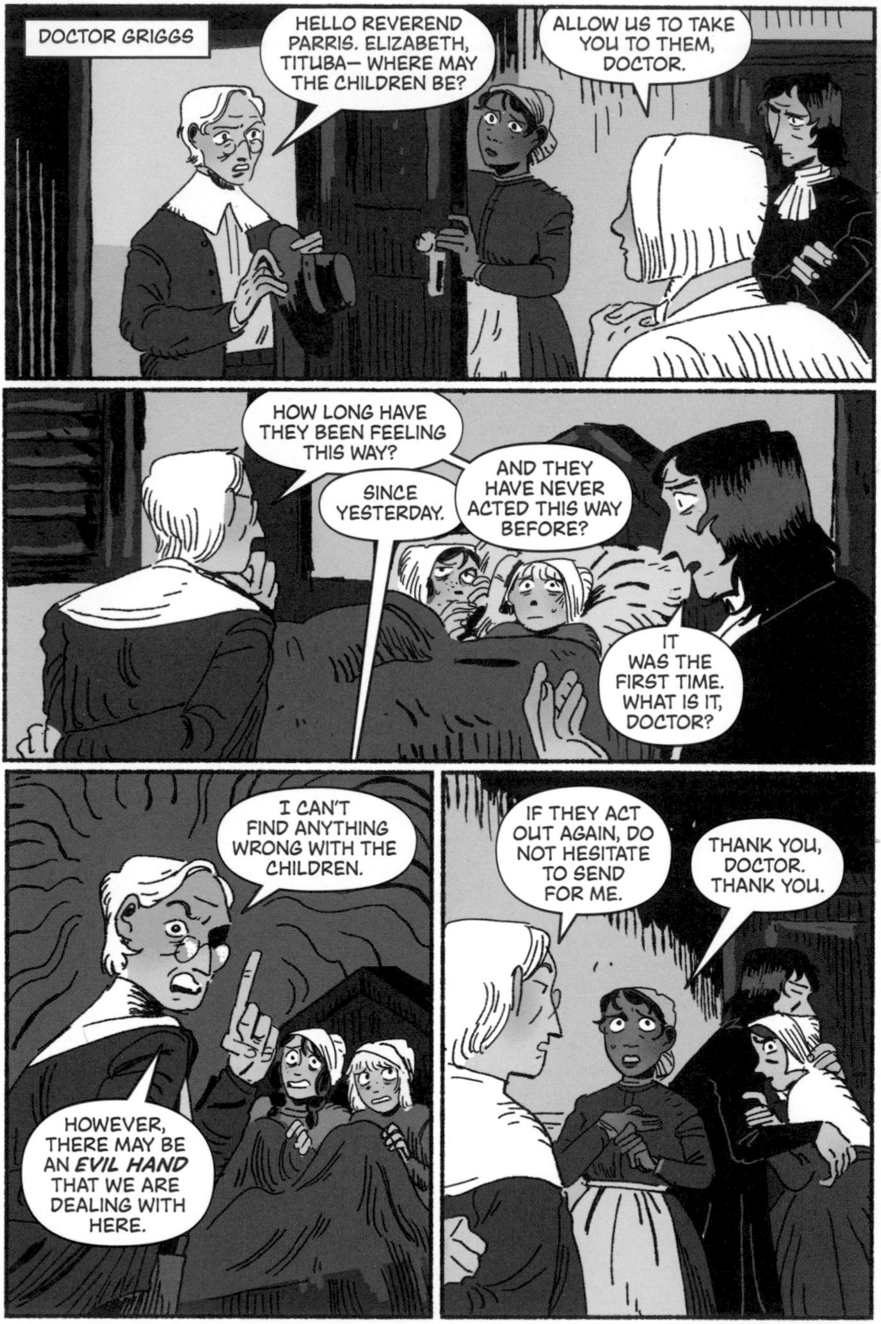
DOCTOR GRIGGS
HELLO REVEREND PARRIS. ELIZABETH, TITUBA— WHERE MAY THE CHILDREN BE?
ALLOW US TO TAKE YOU TO THEM, DOCTOR.
HOW LONG HAVE THEY BEEN FEELING THIS WAY?
SINCE YESTERDAY.
AND THEY HAVE NEVER ACTED THIS WAY BEFORE?
IT WAS THE FIRST TIME. WHAT IS IT, DOCTOR?
I CAN'T FIND ANYTHING WRONG WITH THE CHILDREN.
HOWEVER, THERE MAY BE AN *EVIL HAND* THAT WE ARE DEALING WITH HERE.
IF THEY ACT OUT AGAIN, DO NOT HESITATE TO SEND FOR ME.
THANK YOU, DOCTOR. THANK YOU.

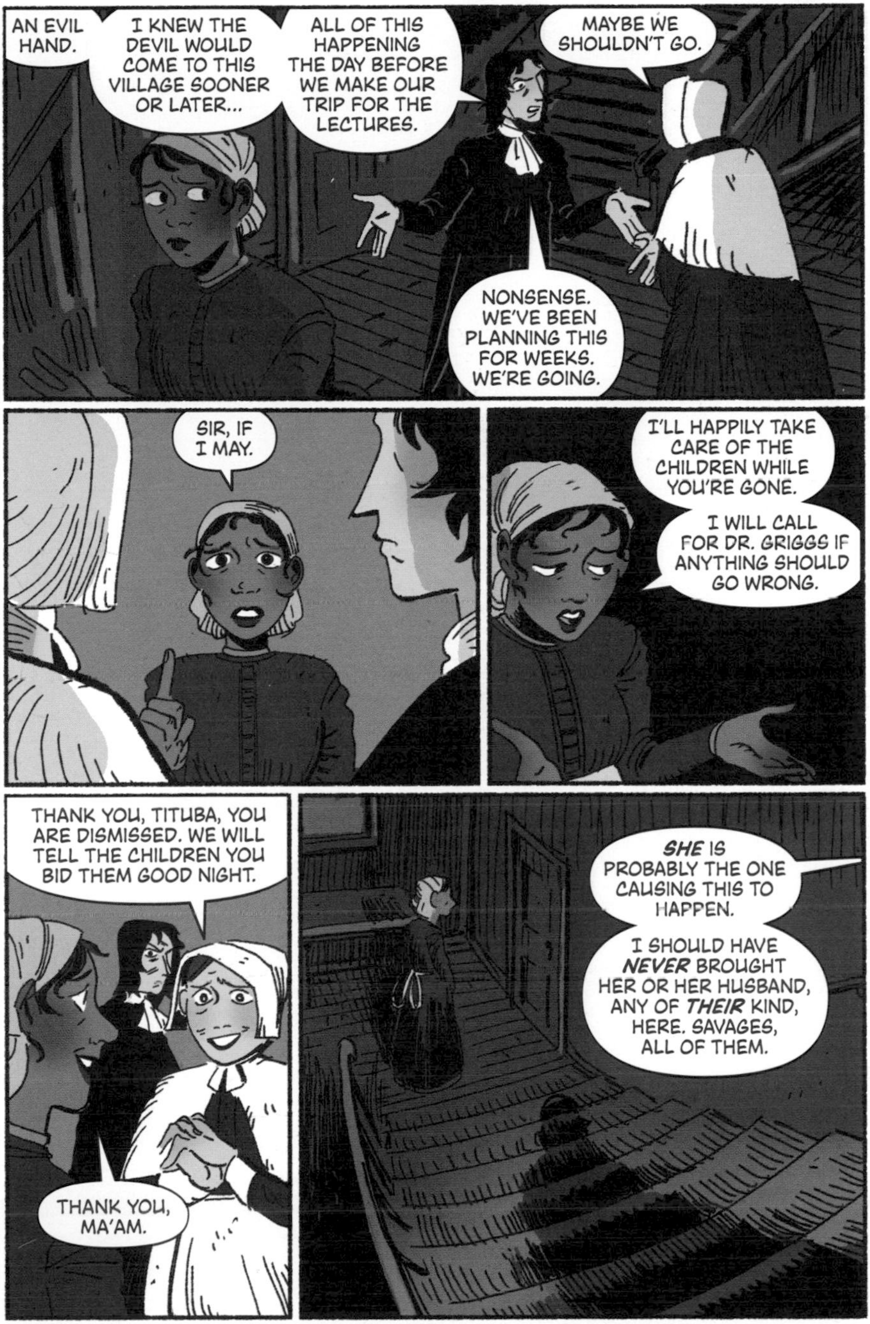
AN EVIL HAND.
I KNEW THE DEVIL WOULD COME TO THIS VILLAGE SOONER OR LATER...
ALL OF THIS HAPPENING THE DAY BEFORE WE MAKE OUR TRIP FOR THE LECTURES.
MAYBE WE SHOULDN'T GO.
NONSENSE. WE'VE BEEN PLANNING THIS FOR WEEKS. WE'RE GOING.
SIR, IF I MAY.
I'LL HAPPILY TAKE CARE OF THE CHILDREN WHILE YOU'RE GONE.
I WILL CALL FOR DR. GRIGGS IF ANYTHING SHOULD GO WRONG.
THANK YOU, TITUBA, YOU ARE DISMISSED. WE WILL TELL THE CHILDREN YOU BID THEM GOOD NIGHT.
THANK YOU, MA'AM.
SHE IS PROBABLY THE ONE CAUSING THIS TO HAPPEN.
I SHOULD HAVE ***NEVER*** BROUGHT HER OR HER HUSBAND, ANY OF ***THEIR*** KIND, HERE. SAVAGES, ALL OF THEM.

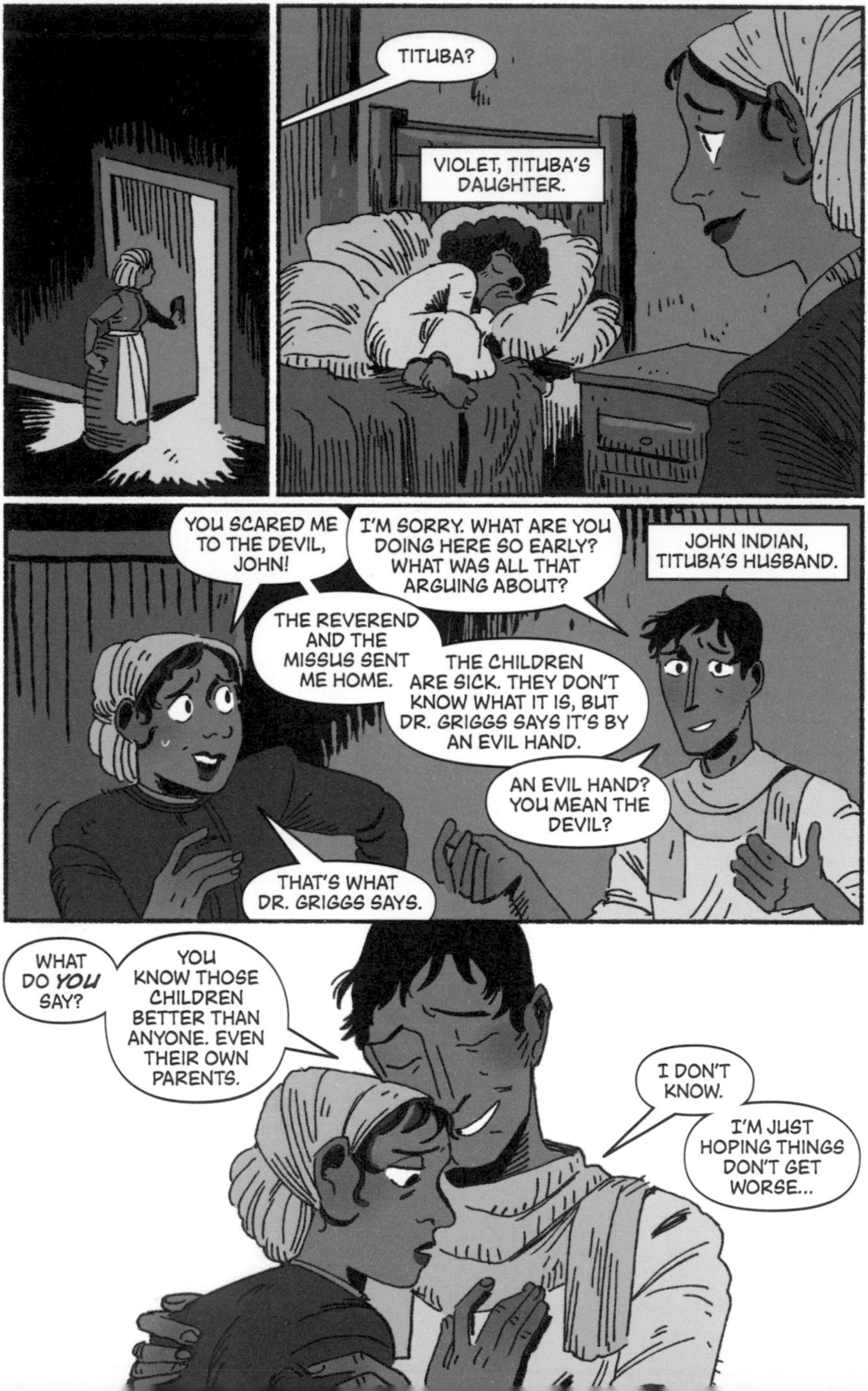
TITUBA?
VIOLET, TITUBA'S DAUGHTER.
YOU SCARED ME TO THE DEVIL, JOHN!
I'M SORRY. WHAT ARE YOU DOING HERE SO EARLY? WHAT WAS ALL THAT ARGUING ABOUT?
JOHN INDIAN, TITUBA'S HUSBAND.
THE REVEREND AND THE MISSUS SENT ME HOME.
THE CHILDREN ARE SICK. THEY DON'T KNOW WHAT IT IS, BUT DR. GRIGGS SAYS IT'S BY AN EVIL HAND.
AN EVIL HAND? YOU MEAN THE DEVIL?
THAT'S WHAT DR. GRIGGS SAYS.
WHAT DO ***YOU*** SAY?
YOU KNOW THOSE CHILDREN BETTER THAN ANYONE. EVEN THEIR OWN PARENTS.
I DON'T KNOW.
I'M JUST HOPING THINGS DON'T GET WORSE...

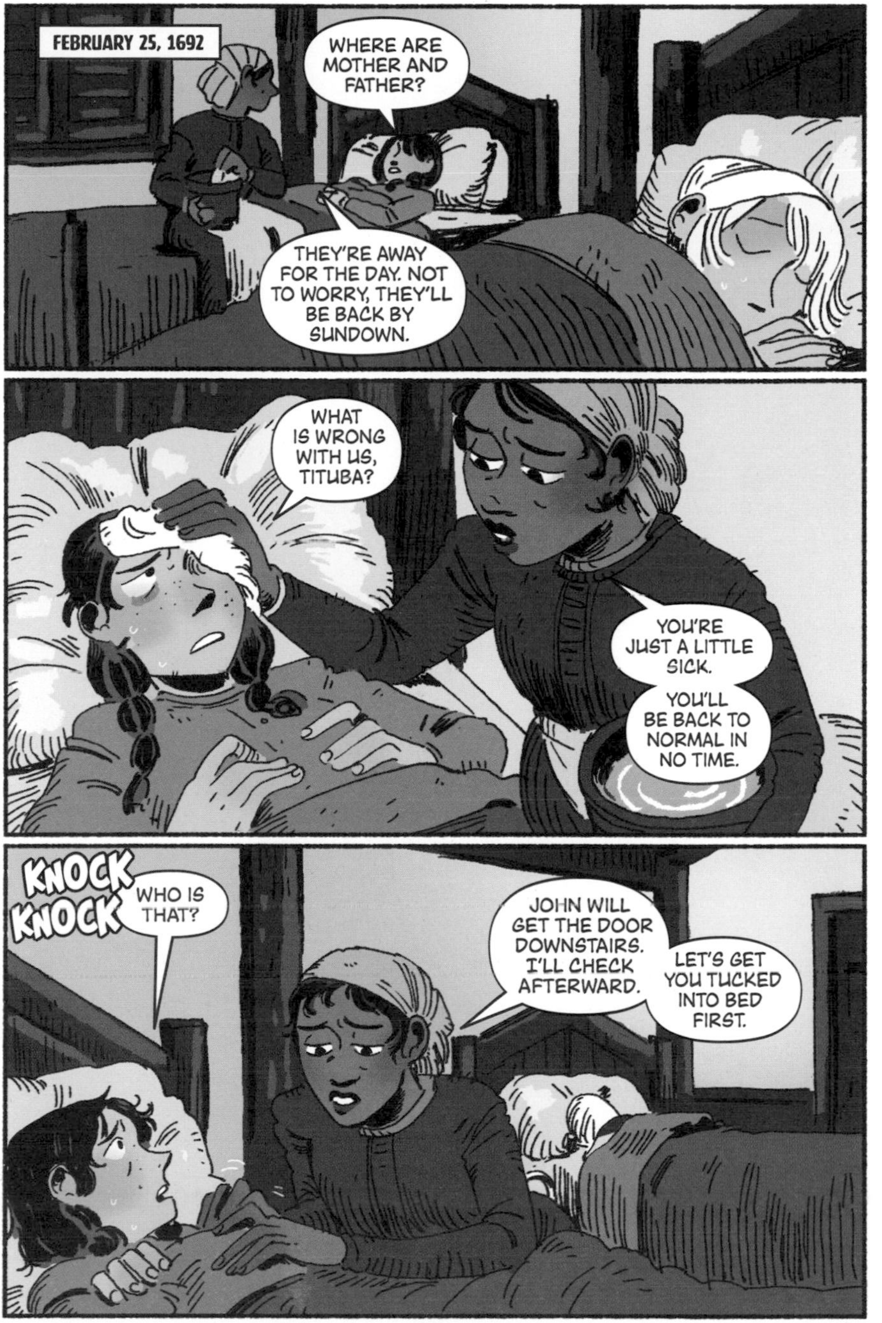
FEBRUARY 25, 1692
WHERE ARE MOTHER AND FATHER?
THEY'RE AWAY FOR THE DAY. NOT TO WORRY, THEY'LL BE BACK BY SUNDOWN.
WHAT IS WRONG WITH US, TITUBA?
YOU'RE JUST A LITTLE SICK.
YOU'LL BE BACK TO NORMAL IN NO TIME.
KNOCK KNOCK
WHO IS THAT?
JOHN WILL GET THE DOOR DOWNSTAIRS. I'LL CHECK AFTERWARD.
LET'S GET YOU TUCKED INTO BED FIRST.

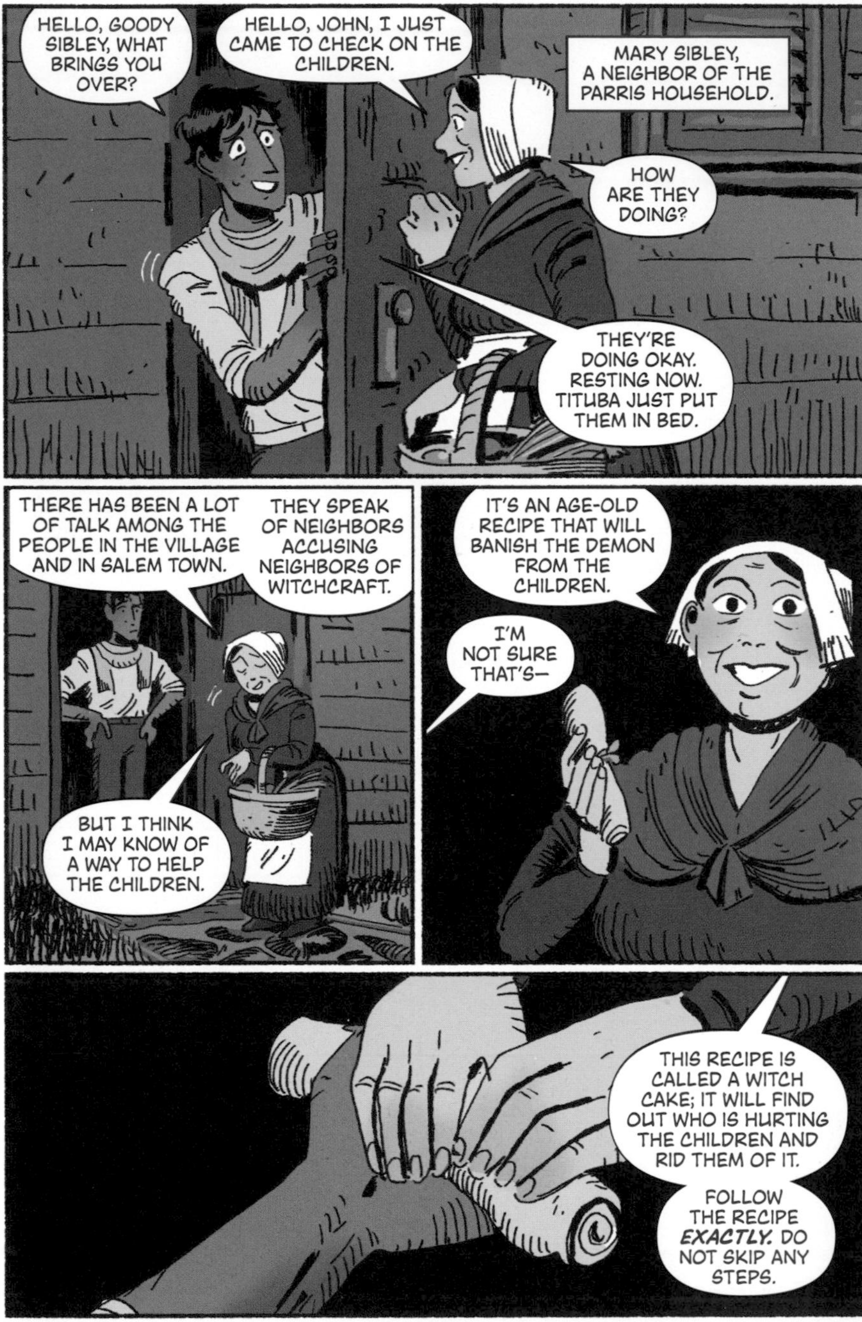
HELLO, GOODY SIBLEY, WHAT BRINGS YOU OVER?
HELLO, JOHN, I JUST CAME TO CHECK ON THE CHILDREN.
MARY SIBLEY, A NEIGHBOR OF THE PARRIS HOUSEHOLD.
HOW ARE THEY DOING?
THEY'RE DOING OKAY. RESTING NOW. TITUBA JUST PUT THEM IN BED.
THERE HAS BEEN A LOT OF TALK AMONG THE PEOPLE IN THE VILLAGE AND IN SALEM TOWN.
THEY SPEAK OF NEIGHBORS ACCUSING NEIGHBORS OF WITCHCRAFT.
BUT I THINK I MAY KNOW OF A WAY TO HELP THE CHILDREN.
IT'S AN AGE-OLD RECIPE THAT WILL BANISH THE DEMON FROM THE CHILDREN.
I'M NOT SURE THAT'S—
THIS RECIPE IS CALLED A WITCH CAKE; IT WILL FIND OUT WHO IS HURTING THE CHILDREN AND RID THEM OF IT.
FOLLOW THE RECIPE ***EXACTLY.*** DO NOT SKIP ANY STEPS.

Witch Cake

A witch cake is a part of traditional English folk magic that was used to identify witches and evildoers. The witch cake was made up of rye-meal (flour) and one other ingredient: the victim's urine, which was believed to be the "witch's essence."

The cake was then baked in the ashes of the fireplace, and once it was ready, it was fed to a dog. Many Puritans thought that dogs were "familiars" to witches. Familiars (or imps) known as "witch attendants" were thought to be creatures who would help with the witch's spells and protect them if needed. A familiar could be any animal, including a rat, a cat, or a dog.

It was believed that once the dog bit into the cake, the witch would either feel every bite and stop their sinful misdeeds or the dog would reveal the witch's name with a bark. This practice was later condemned by Reverend Parris and the Puritan Church.

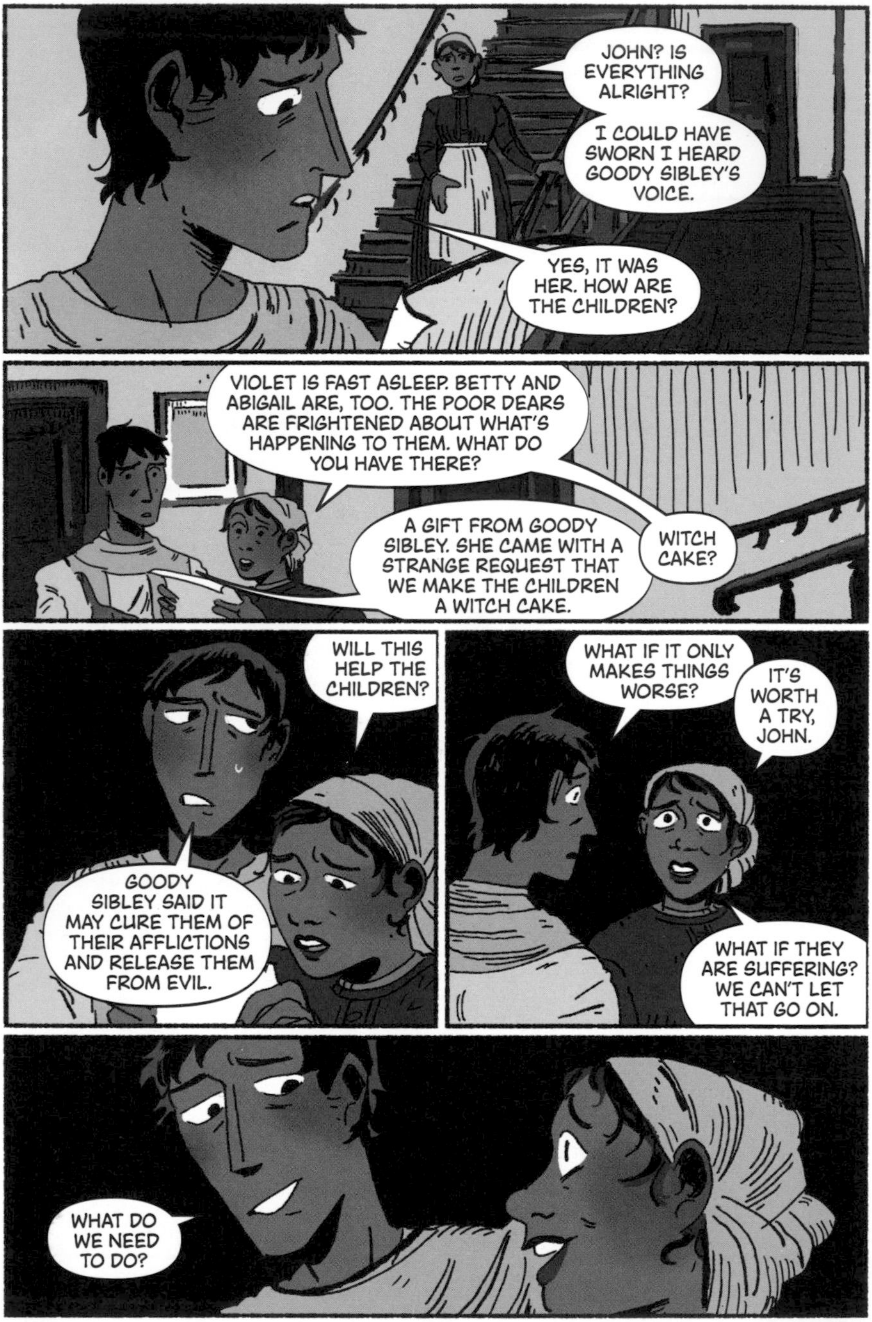
JOHN? IS EVERYTHING ALRIGHT?
I COULD HAVE SWORN I HEARD GOODY SIBLEY'S VOICE.
YES, IT WAS HER. HOW ARE THE CHILDREN?
VIOLET IS FAST ASLEEP. BETTY AND ABIGAIL ARE, TOO. THE POOR DEARS ARE FRIGHTENED ABOUT WHAT'S HAPPENING TO THEM. WHAT DO YOU HAVE THERE?
A GIFT FROM GOODY SIBLEY. SHE CAME WITH A STRANGE REQUEST THAT WE MAKE THE CHILDREN A WITCH CAKE.
WITCH CAKE?
WILL THIS HELP THE CHILDREN?
GOODY SIBLEY SAID IT MAY CURE THEM OF THEIR AFFLICTIONS AND RELEASE THEM FROM EVIL.
WHAT IF IT ONLY MAKES THINGS WORSE?
IT'S WORTH A TRY, JOHN.
WHAT IF THEY ARE SUFFERING? WE CAN'T LET THAT GO ON.
WHAT DO WE NEED TO DO?

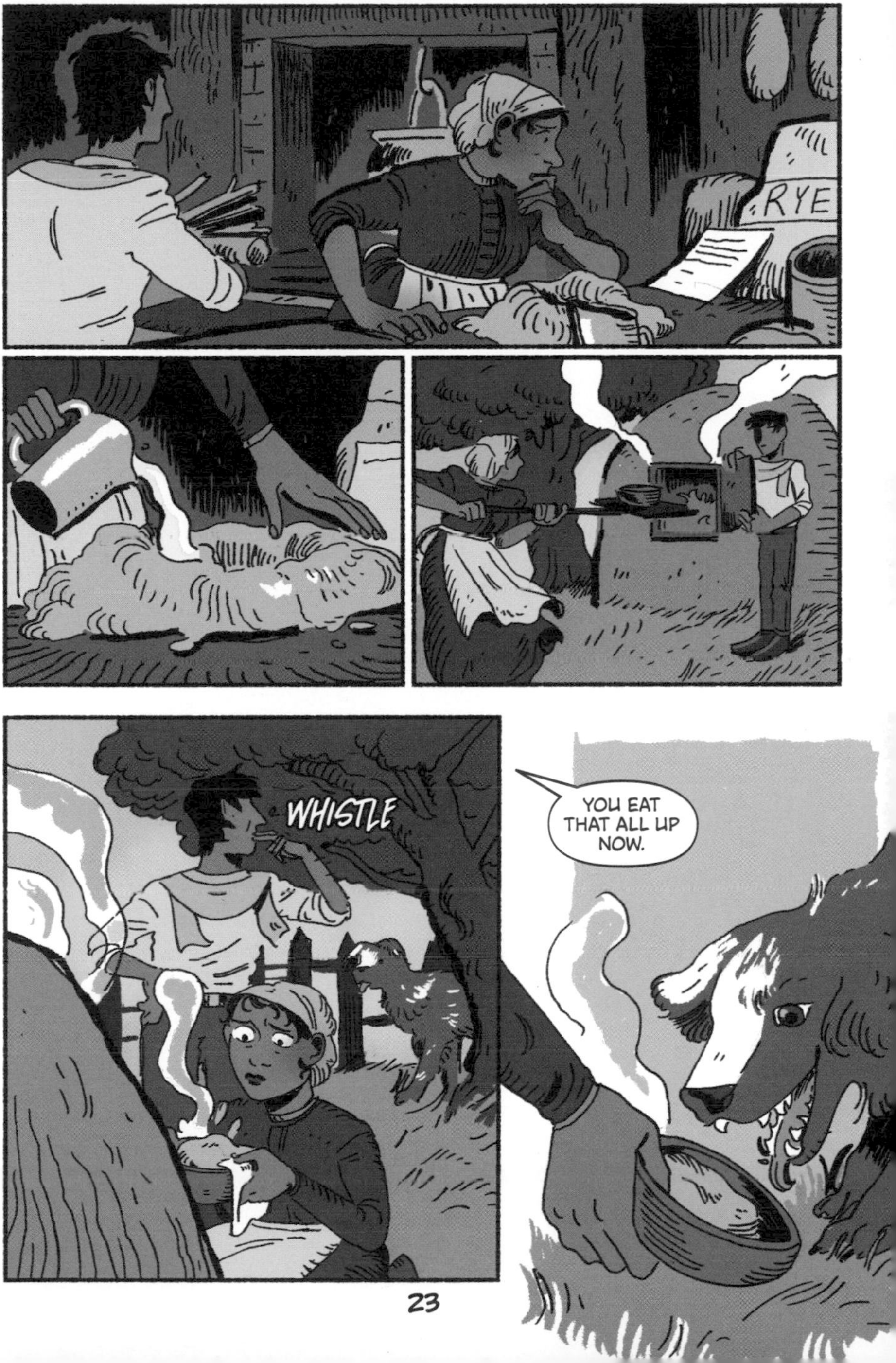
RYE
WHISTLE
YOU EAT THAT ALL UP NOW.

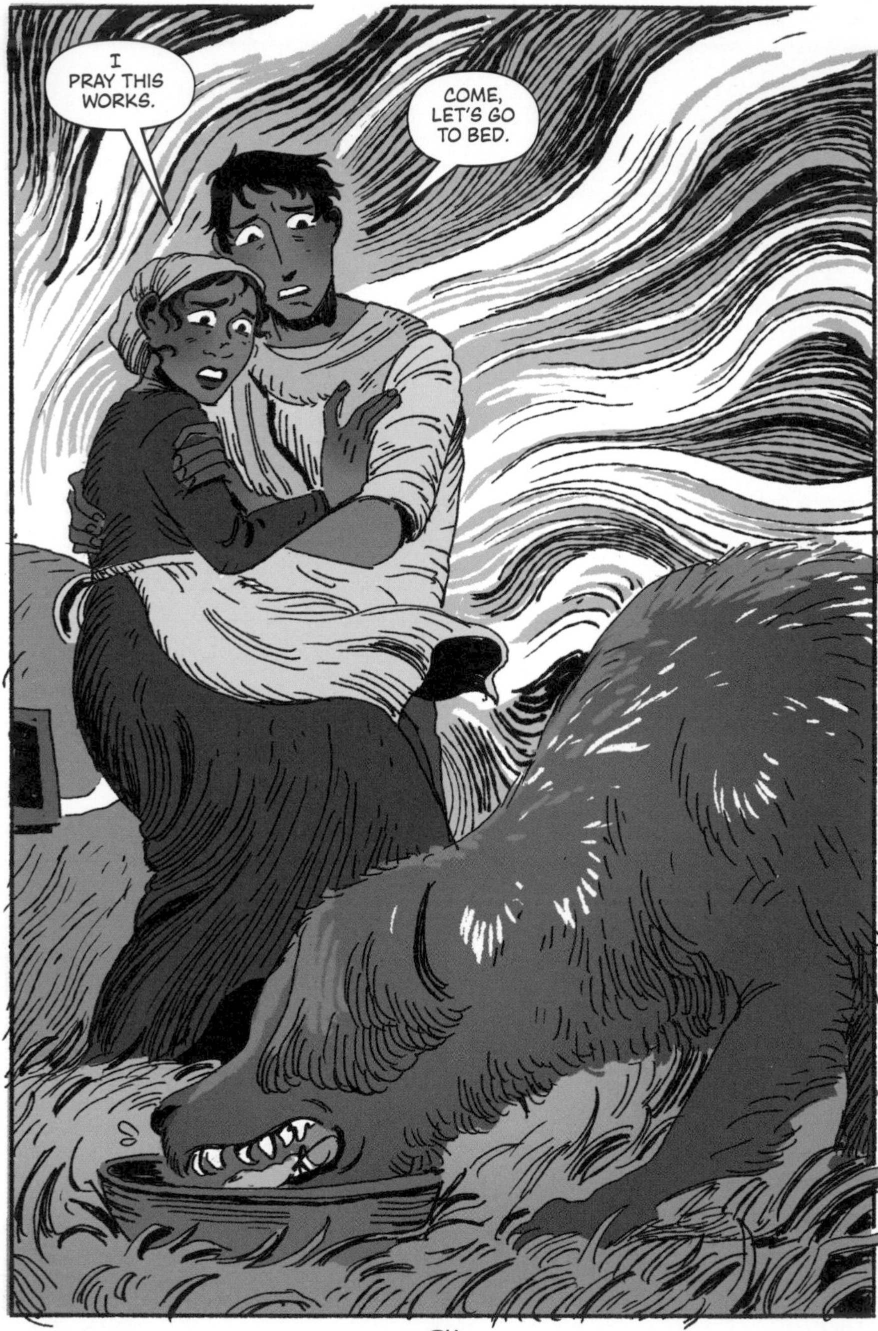
I PRAY THIS WORKS.
COME, LET'S GO TO BED.

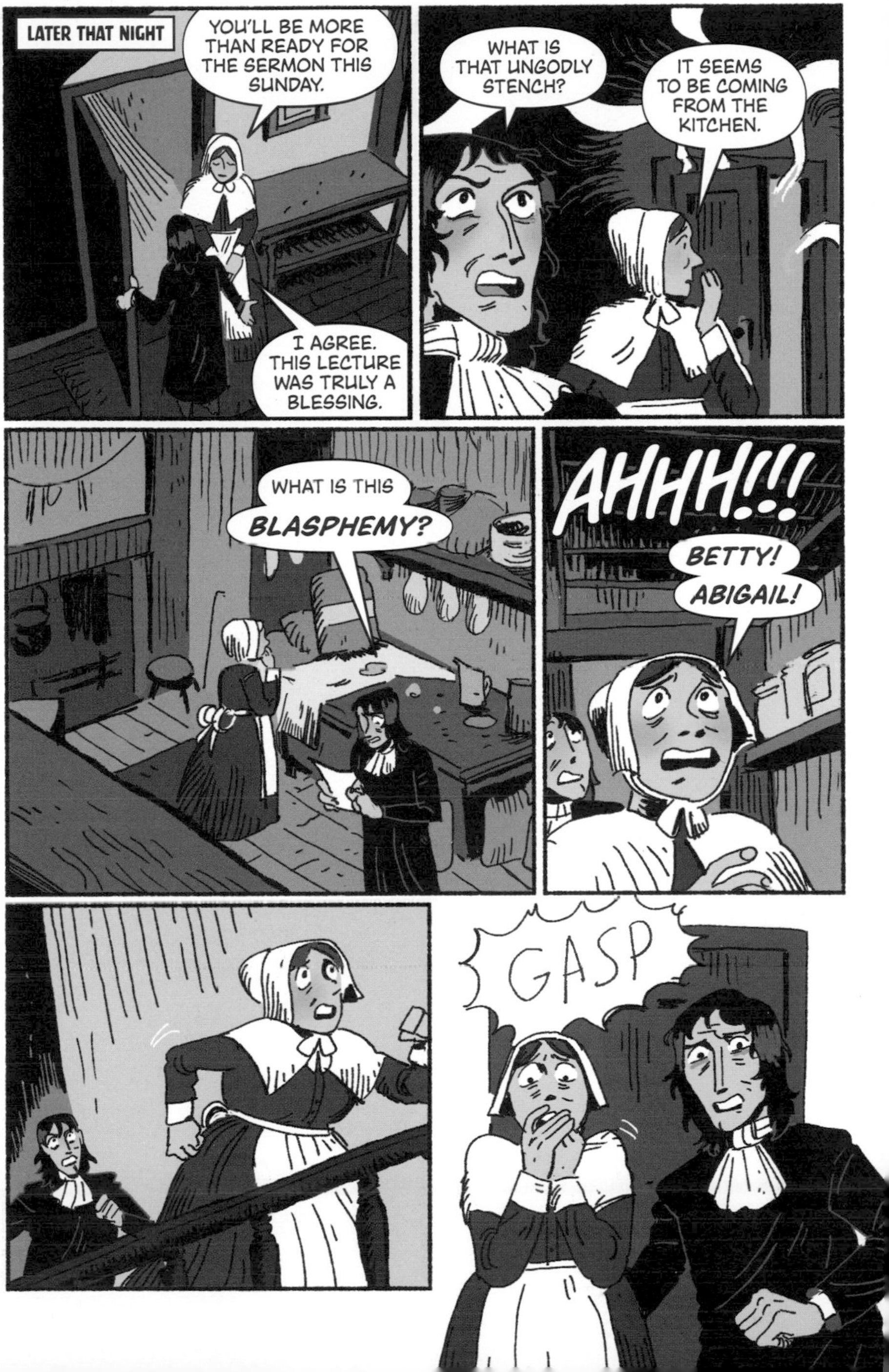
LATER THAT NIGHT
YOU'LL BE MORE THAN READY FOR THE SERMON THIS SUNDAY.
I AGREE. THIS LECTURE WAS TRULY A BLESSING.
WHAT IS THAT UNGODLY STENCH?
IT SEEMS TO BE COMING FROM THE KITCHEN.
WHAT IS THIS BLASPHEMY?
AHHH!!!
BETTY! ABIGAIL!
GASP

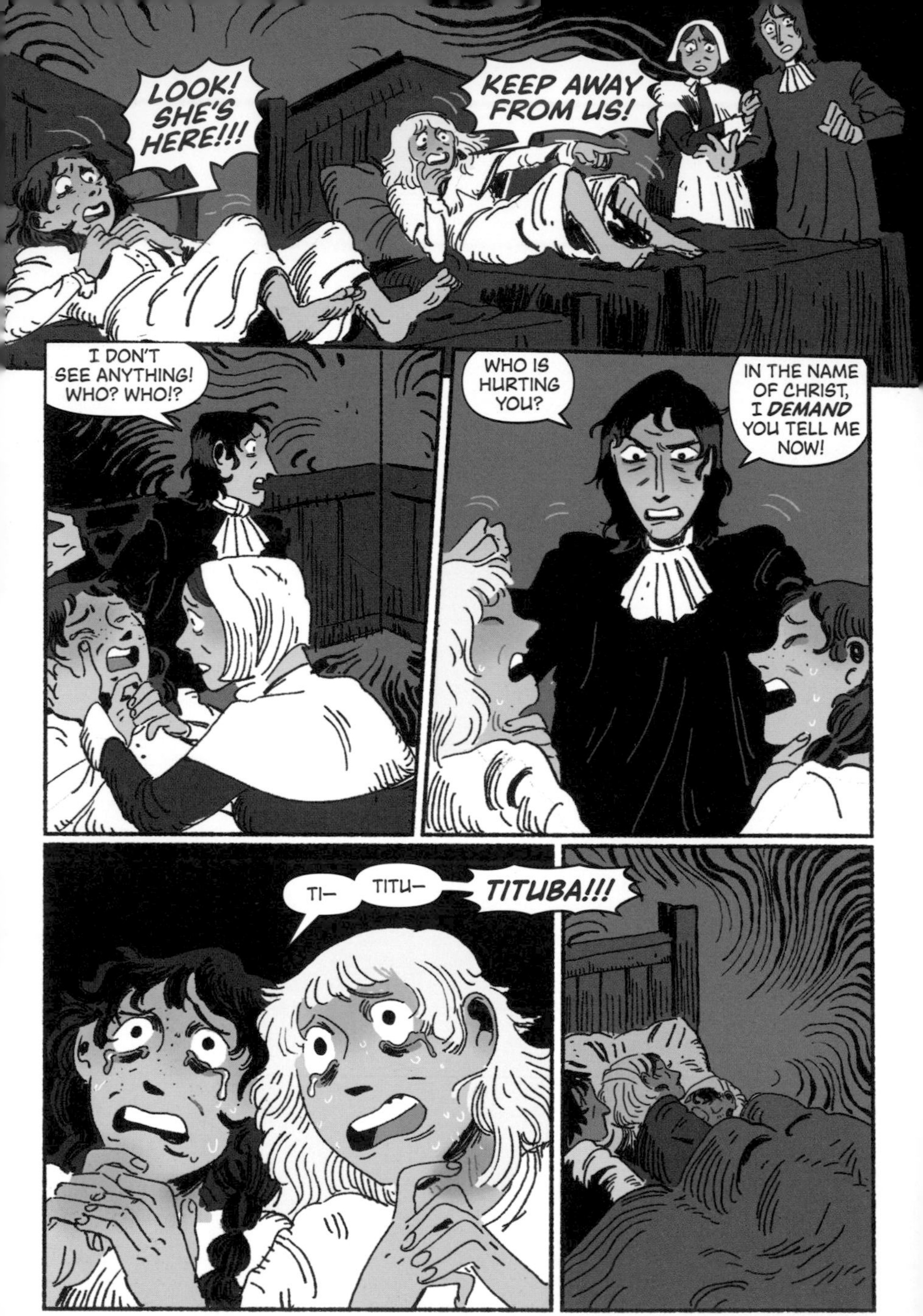
LOOK! SHE'S HERE!!!
KEEP AWAY FROM US!
I DON'T SEE ANYTHING! WHO? WHO!?
WHO IS HURTING YOU?
IN THE NAME OF CHRIST, I *DEMAND* YOU TELL ME NOW!
TI—
TITU—
TITUBA!!!

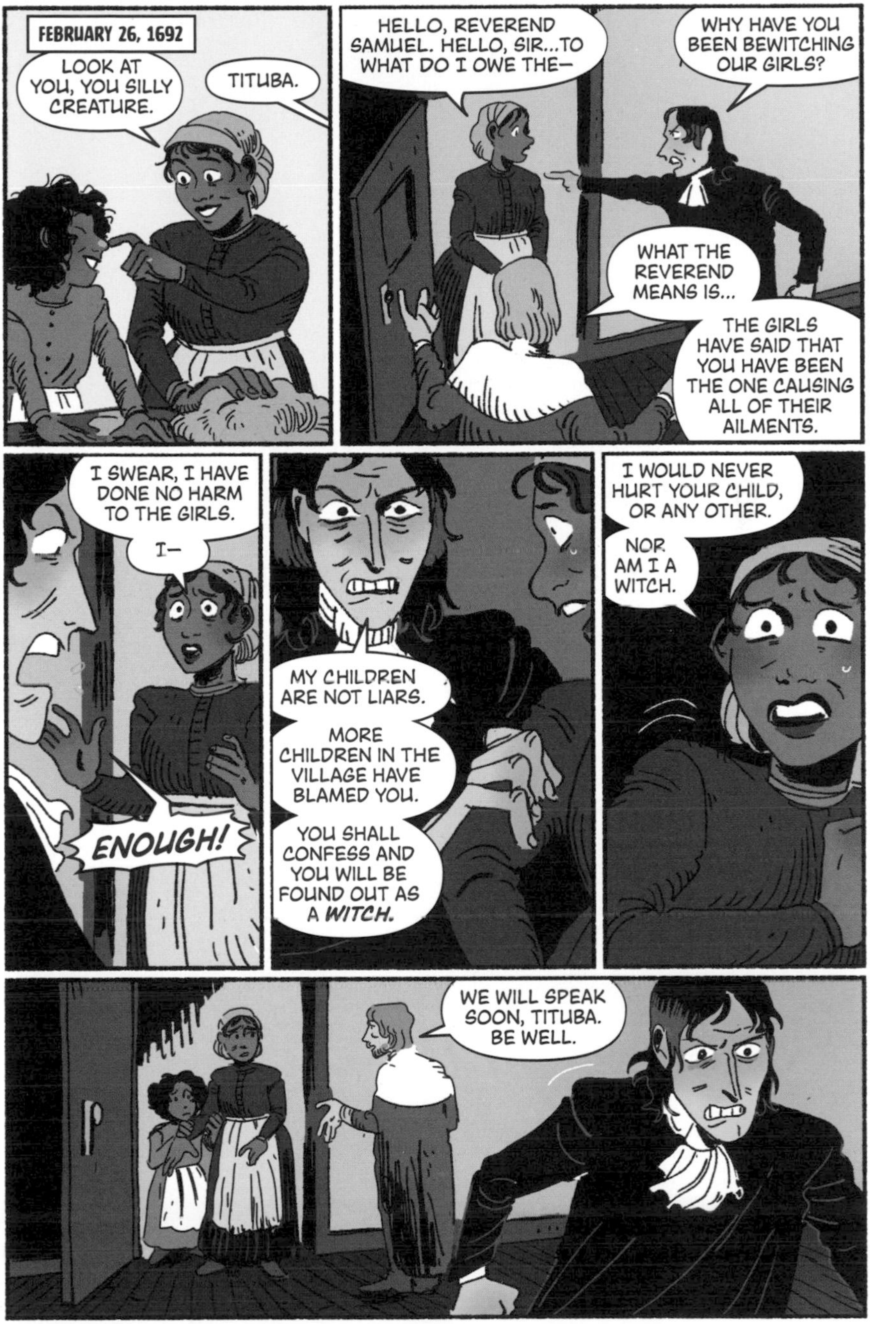
FEBRUARY 26, 1692
LOOK AT YOU, YOU SILLY CREATURE.
TITUBA.
HELLO, REVEREND SAMUEL. HELLO, SIR...TO WHAT DO I OWE THE—
WHY HAVE YOU BEEN BEWITCHING OUR GIRLS?
WHAT THE REVEREND MEANS IS...
THE GIRLS HAVE SAID THAT YOU HAVE BEEN THE ONE CAUSING ALL OF THEIR AILMENTS.
I SWEAR, I HAVE DONE NO HARM TO THE GIRLS.
I—
ENOUGH!
MY CHILDREN ARE NOT LIARS.
MORE CHILDREN IN THE VILLAGE HAVE BLAMED YOU.
YOU SHALL CONFESS AND YOU WILL BE FOUND OUT AS A *WITCH*.
I WOULD NEVER HURT YOUR CHILD, OR ANY OTHER.
NOR AM I A WITCH.
WE WILL SPEAK SOON, TITUBA. BE WELL.

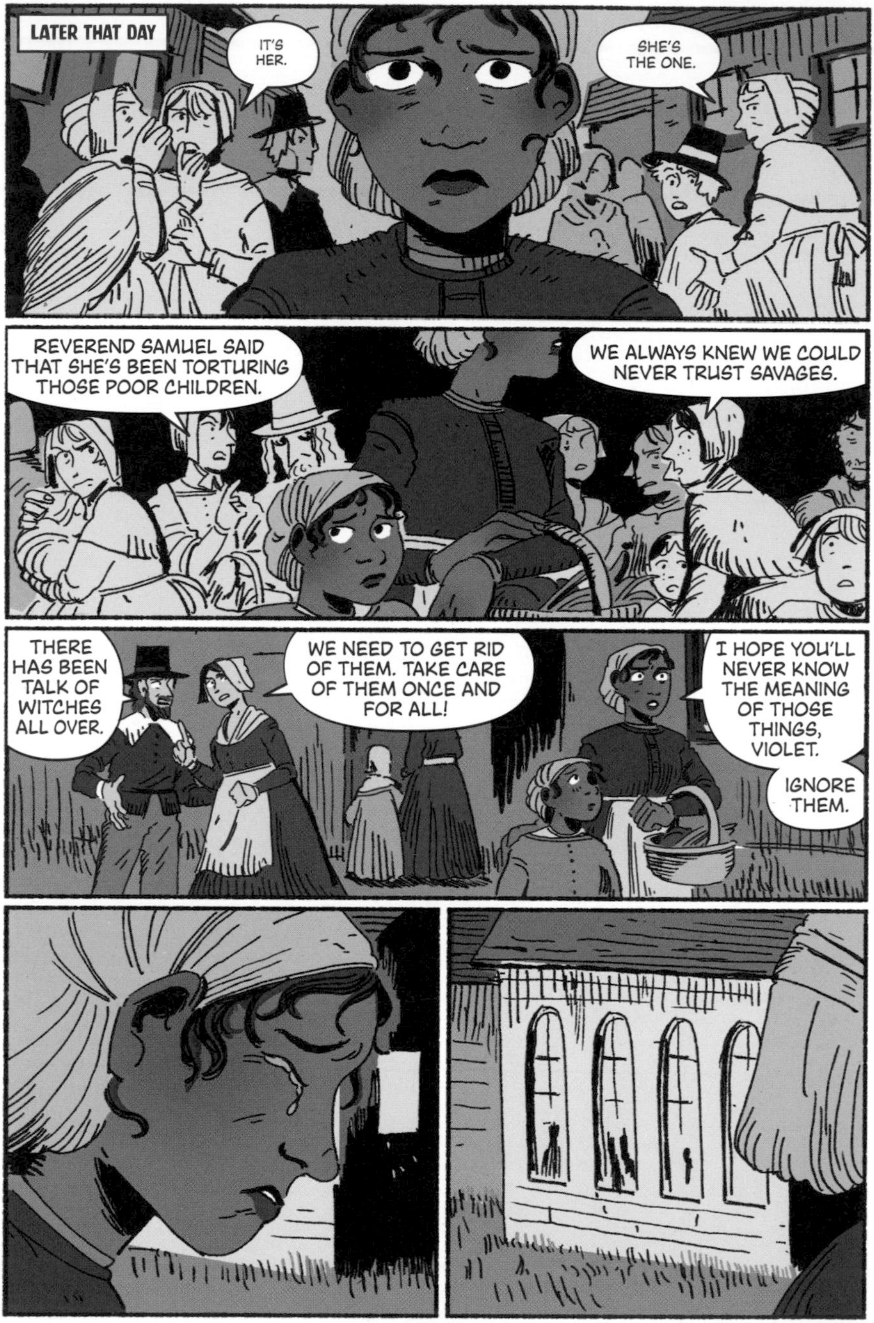
LATER THAT DAY
IT'S HER.
SHE'S THE ONE.
REVEREND SAMUEL SAID THAT SHE'S BEEN TORTURING THOSE POOR CHILDREN.
WE ALWAYS KNEW WE COULD NEVER TRUST SAVAGES.
THERE HAS BEEN TALK OF WITCHES ALL OVER.
WE NEED TO GET RID OF THEM. TAKE CARE OF THEM ONCE AND FOR ALL!
I HOPE YOU'LL NEVER KNOW THE MEANING OF THOSE THINGS, VIOLET.
IGNORE THEM.

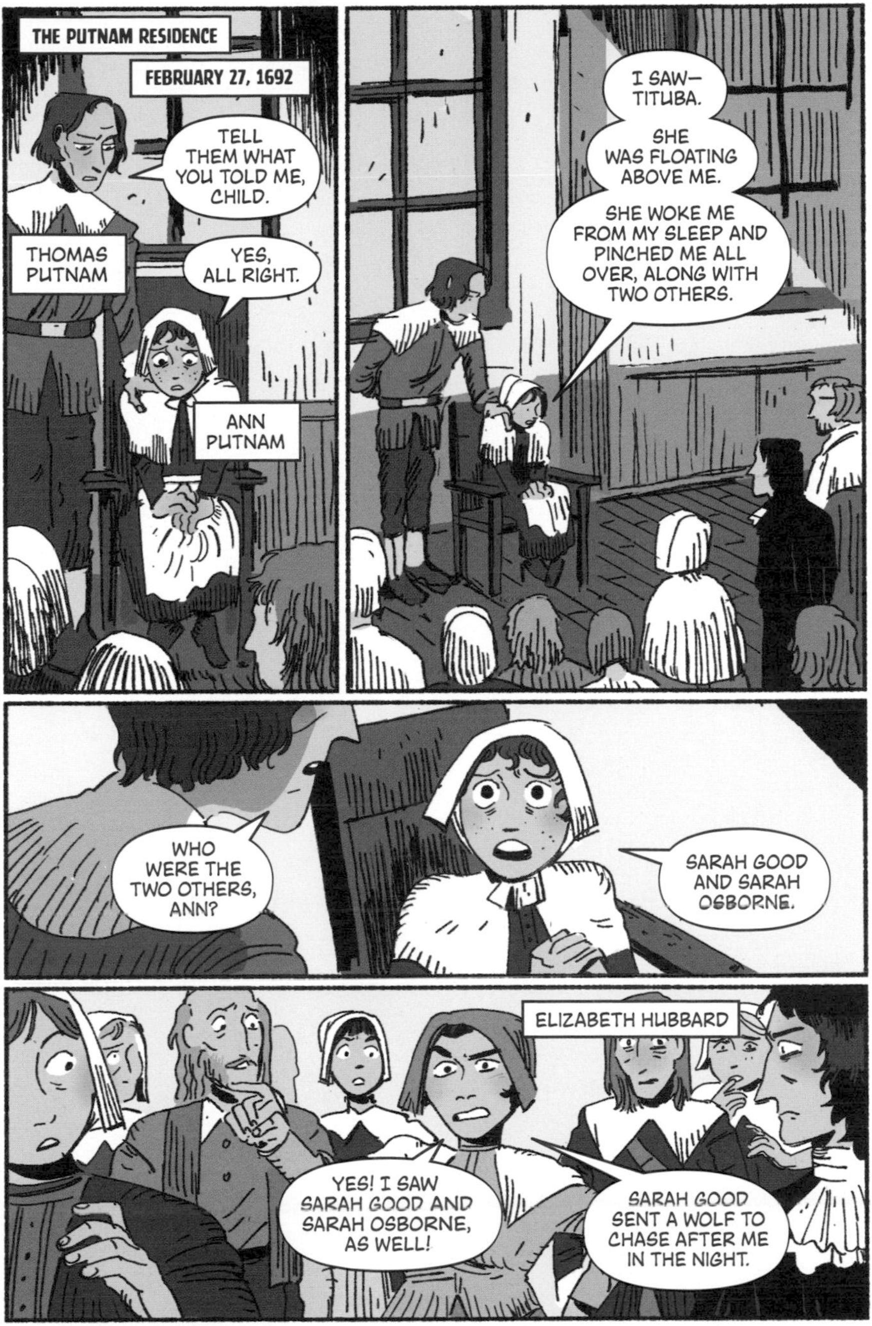
THE PUTNAM RESIDENCE
FEBRUARY 27, 1692
TELL THEM WHAT YOU TOLD ME, CHILD.
THOMAS PUTNAM
YES, ALL RIGHT.
ANN PUTNAM
I SAW— TITUBA.
SHE WAS FLOATING ABOVE ME.
SHE WOKE ME FROM MY SLEEP AND PINCHED ME ALL OVER, ALONG WITH TWO OTHERS.
WHO WERE THE TWO OTHERS, ANN?
SARAH GOOD AND SARAH OSBORNE.
ELIZABETH HUBBARD
YES! I SAW SARAH GOOD AND SARAH OSBORNE, AS WELL!
SARAH GOOD SENT A WOLF TO CHASE AFTER ME IN THE NIGHT.

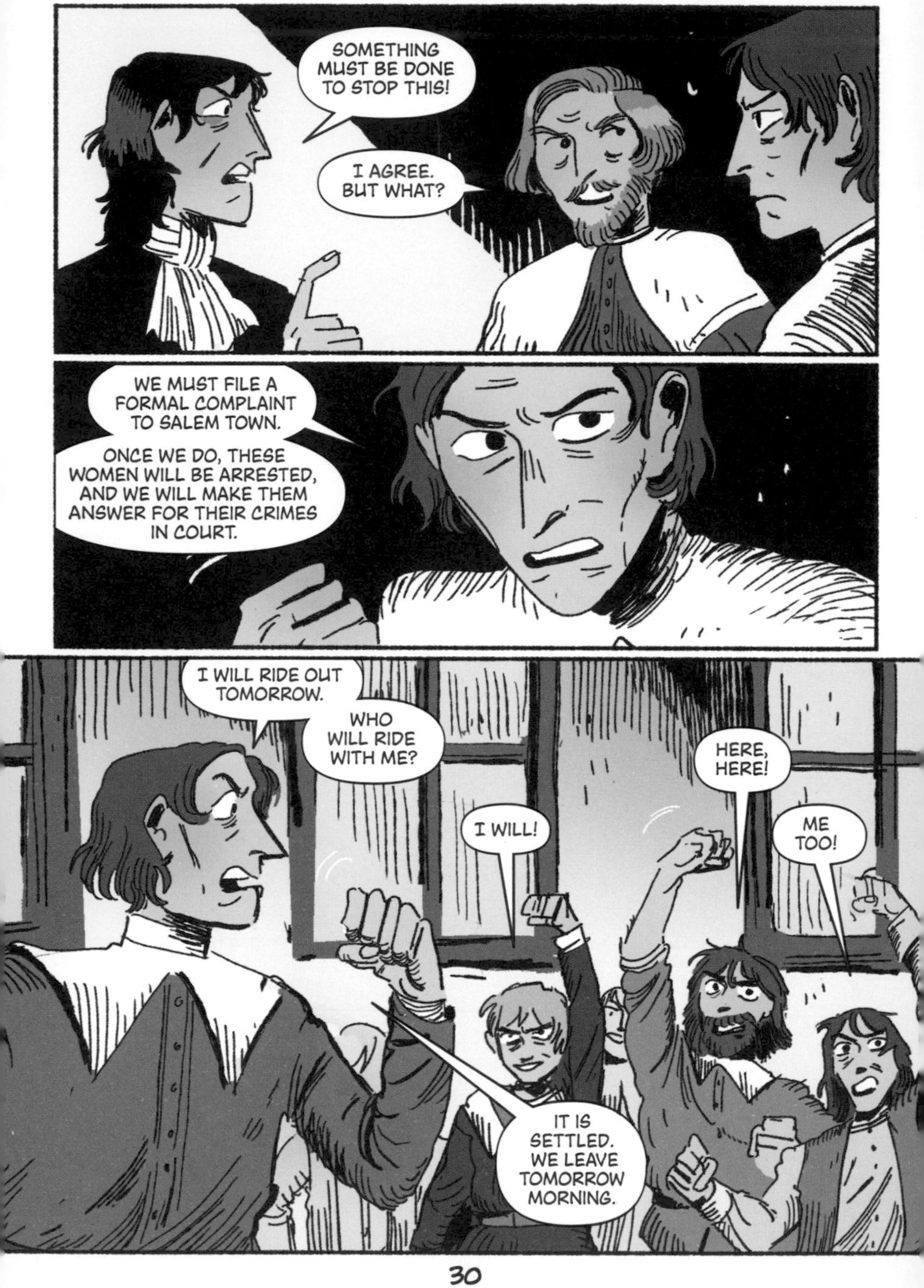
SOMETHING MUST BE DONE TO STOP THIS!
I AGREE. BUT WHAT?
WE MUST FILE A FORMAL COMPLAINT TO SALEM TOWN.
ONCE WE DO, THESE WOMEN WILL BE ARRESTED, AND WE WILL MAKE THEM ANSWER FOR THEIR CRIMES IN COURT.
I WILL RIDE OUT TOMORROW.
WHO WILL RIDE WITH ME?
HERE, HERE!
I WILL!
ME TOO!
IT IS SETTLED. WE LEAVE TOMORROW MORNING.

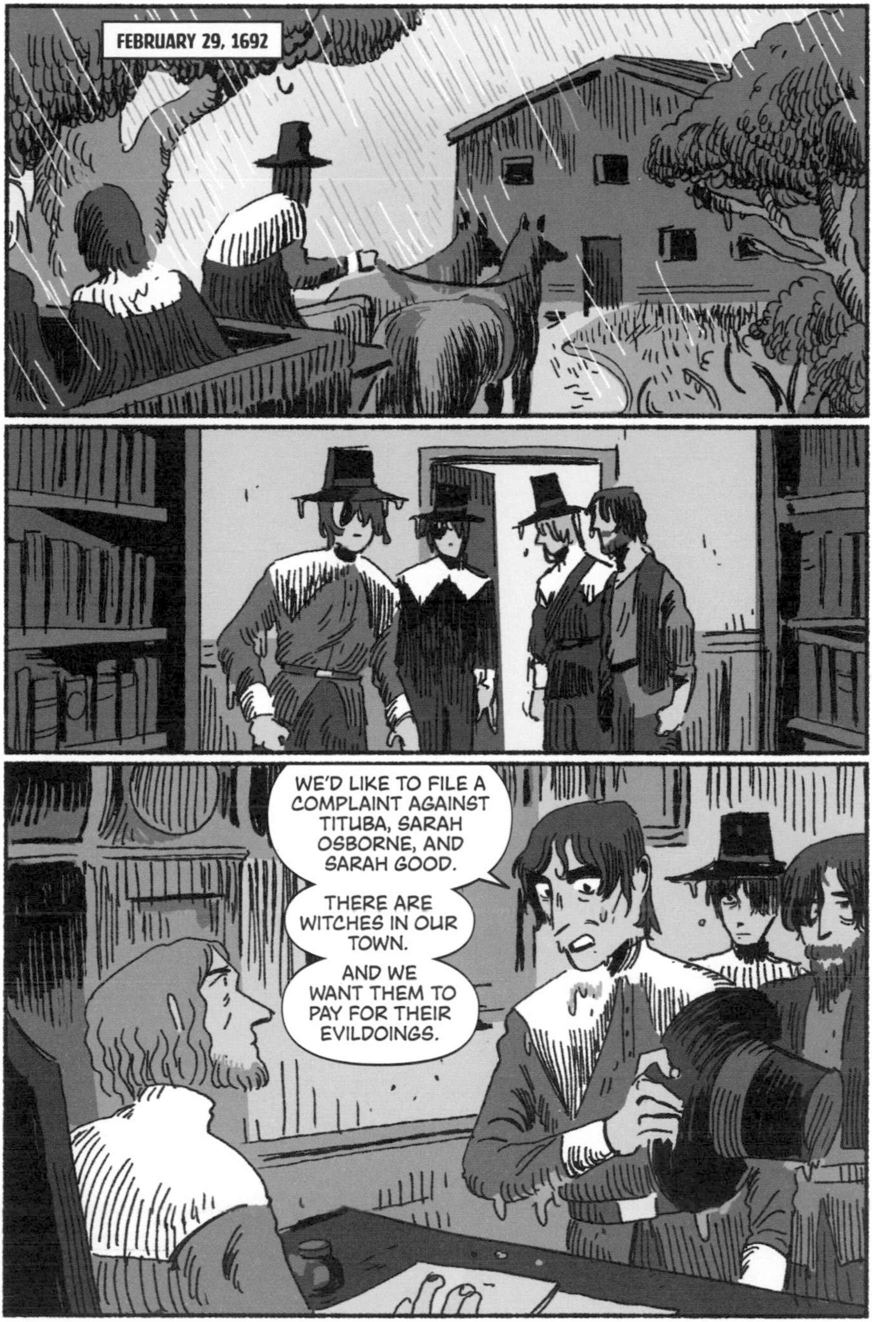
FEBRUARY 29, 1692
WE'D LIKE TO FILE A COMPLAINT AGAINST TITUBA, SARAH OSBORNE, AND SARAH GOOD.
THERE ARE WITCHES IN OUR TOWN.
AND WE WANT THEM TO PAY FOR THEIR EVILDOINGS.

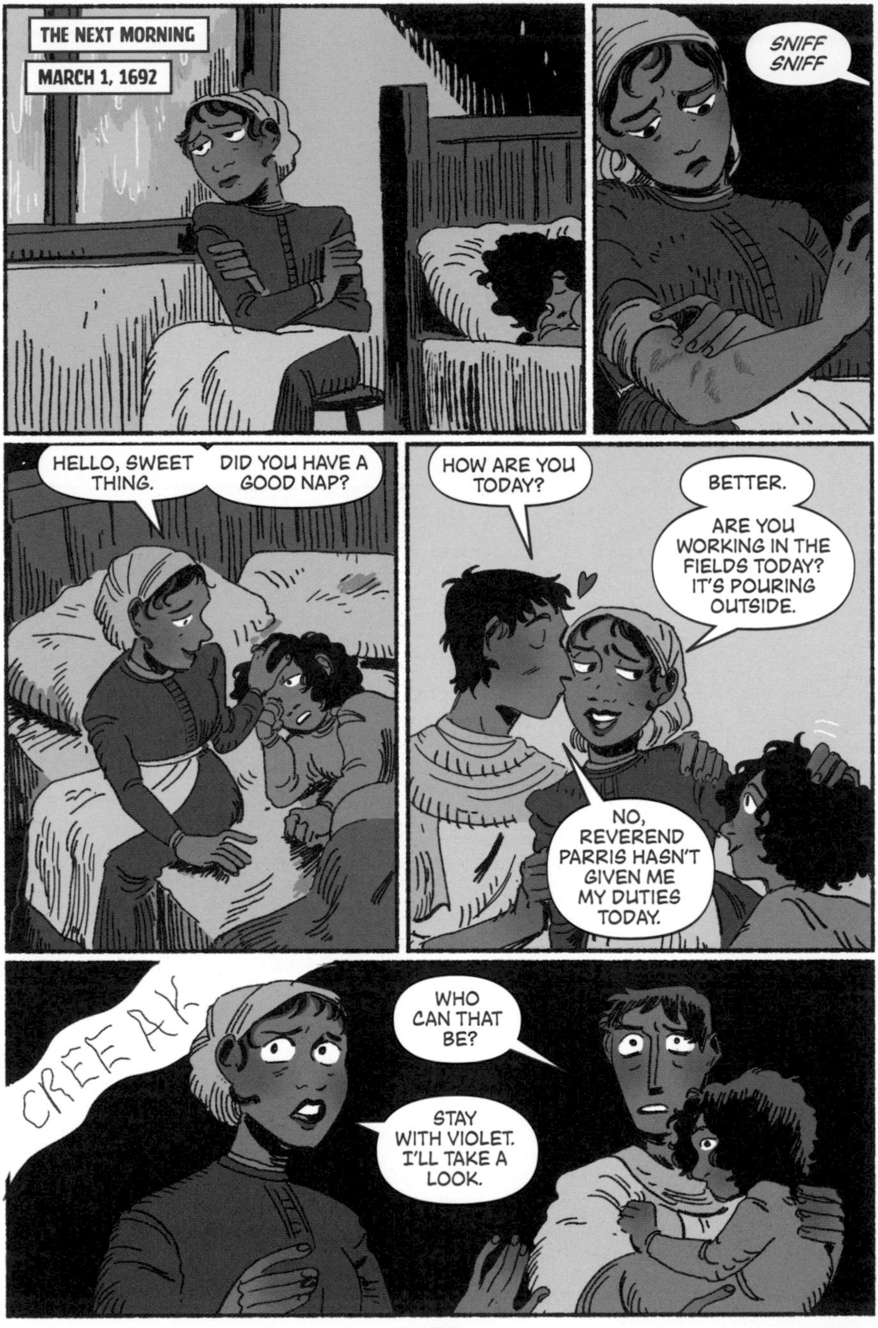
THE NEXT MORNING
MARCH 1, 1692
SNIFF SNIFF
HELLO, SWEET THING.
DID YOU HAVE A GOOD NAP?
HOW ARE YOU TODAY?
BETTER.
ARE YOU WORKING IN THE FIELDS TODAY? IT'S POURING OUTSIDE.
NO, REVEREND PARRIS HASN'T GIVEN ME MY DUTIES TODAY.
CREEAK
WHO CAN THAT BE?
STAY WITH VIOLET. I'LL TAKE A LOOK.

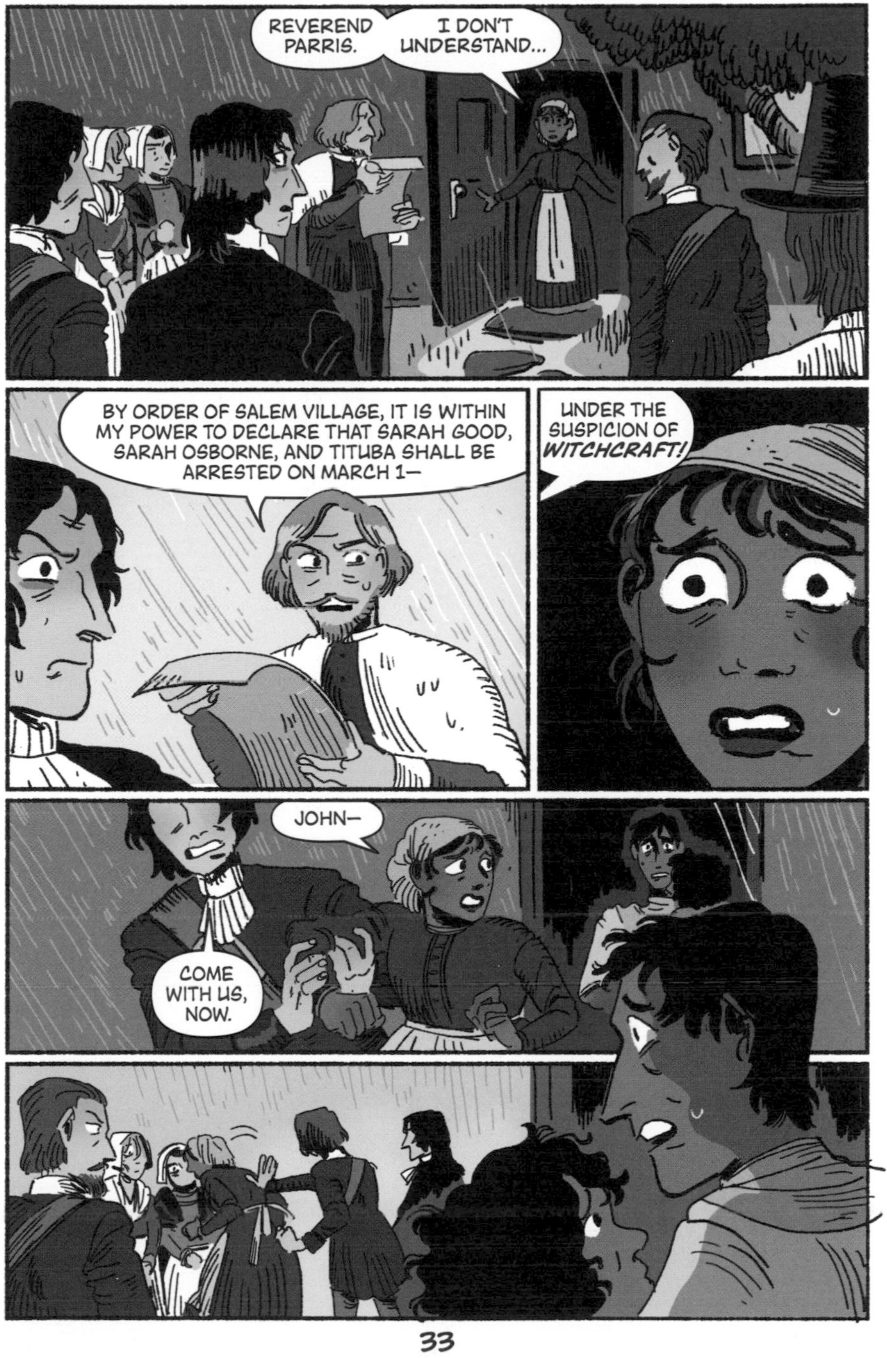
REVEREND PARRIS.
I DON'T UNDERSTAND...
BY ORDER OF SALEM VILLAGE, IT IS WITHIN MY POWER TO DECLARE THAT SARAH GOOD, SARAH OSBORNE, AND TITUBA SHALL BE ARRESTED ON MARCH 1—
UNDER THE SUSPICION OF *WITCHCRAFT!*
JOHN—
COME WITH US, NOW.

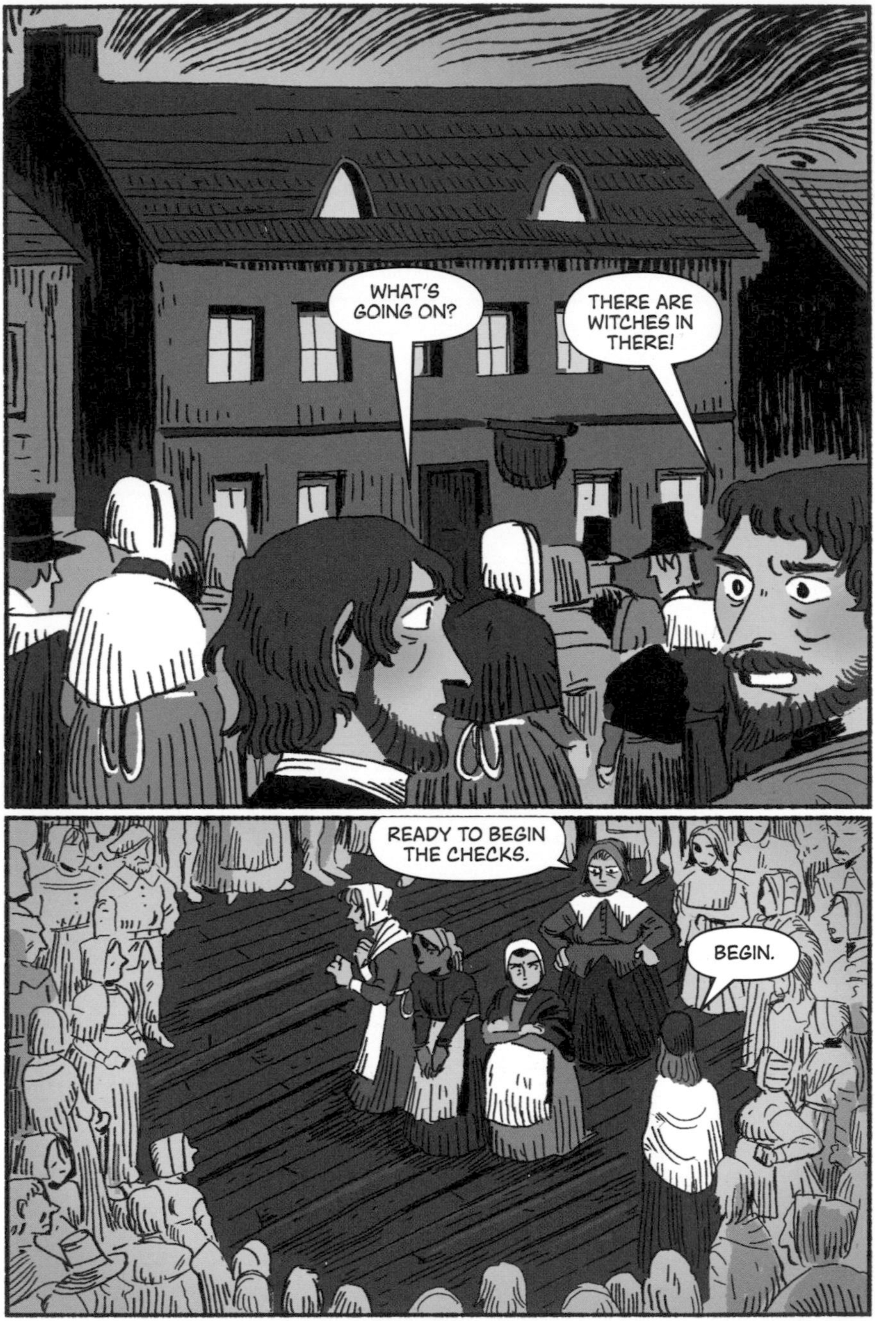
WHAT'S GOING ON?
THERE ARE WITCHES IN THERE!
READY TO BEGIN THE CHECKS.
BEGIN.

How to Spot a Witch

In Puritan communities, witch-hunters believed that a witch could be spotted by doing a number of different trials or "tests." For instance, many suspects were checked for any strange moles, scars, or birthmarks—and even asked about their dreams. If witch-hunters found any of these marks or dreams to be unusual, the accused were deemed to be witches.

Many suspects were often asked to do a "prayer test." It was believed that witches couldn't speak scripture without making mistakes, so the accused were asked to recite passages from the Bible to prove their innocence. For some, it was easy. For others, especially those who could not read, had a speech problem, or were simply nervous, it was an impossible feat.

The ways to spot a witch were also sometimes deadly. One trial in particular was known as the "swimming test": The accused would be thrown into a body of water to see if they would sink or float. Because witches weren't baptized, many believed that the water would allow them to float. An innocent, baptized person, on the other hand, would sink into the water and drown.

These tests would later be proven to exploit people's vulnerabilities and weaknesses, and were specifically set up as a disadvantage to the suspects.

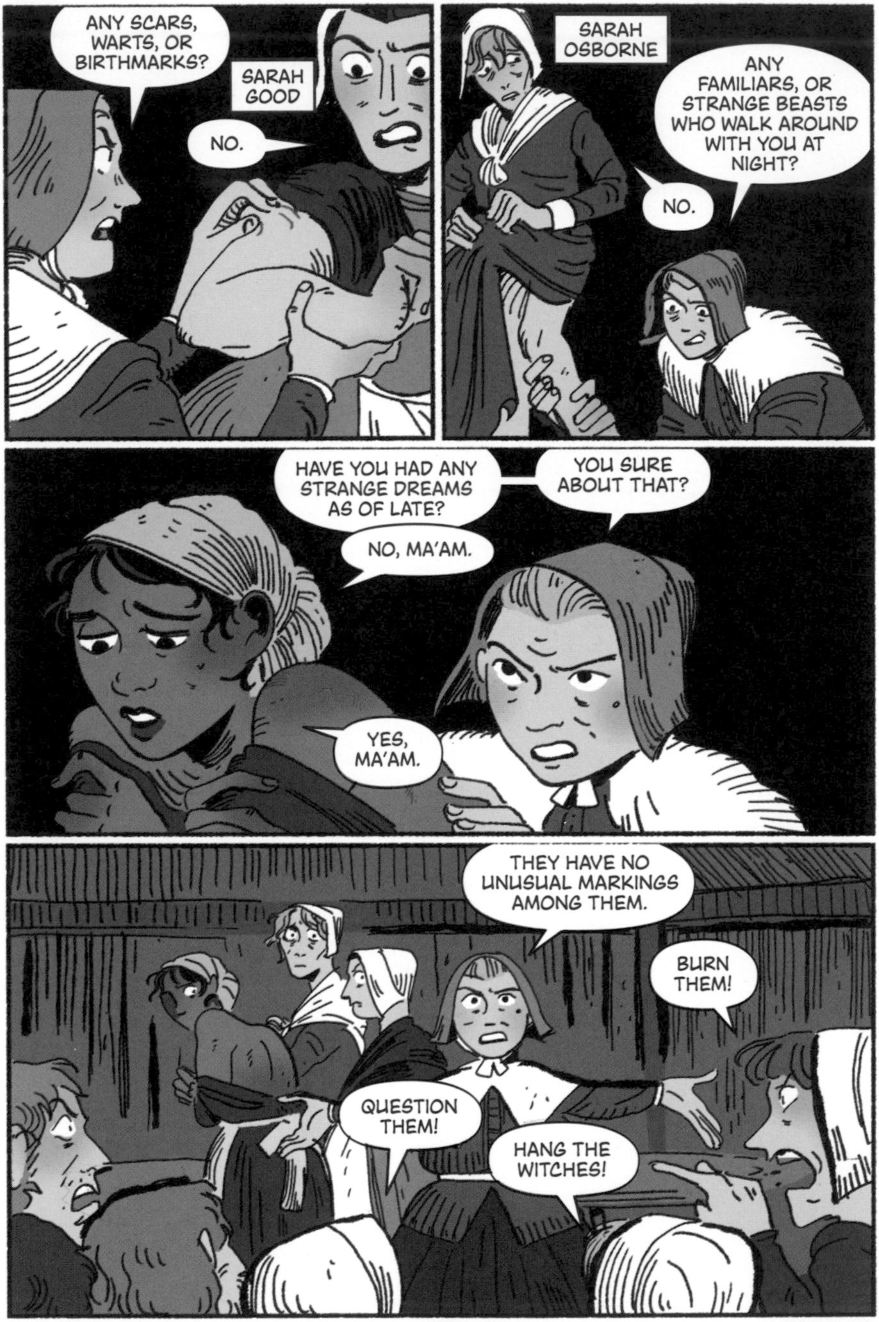
ANY SCARS, WARTS, OR BIRTHMARKS?
SARAH GOOD
NO.
SARAH OSBORNE
ANY FAMILIARS, OR STRANGE BEASTS WHO WALK AROUND WITH YOU AT NIGHT?
NO.
HAVE YOU HAD ANY STRANGE DREAMS AS OF LATE?
NO, MA'AM.
YOU SURE ABOUT THAT?
YES, MA'AM.
THEY HAVE NO UNUSUAL MARKINGS AMONG THEM.
BURN THEM!
QUESTION THEM!
HANG THE WITCHES!

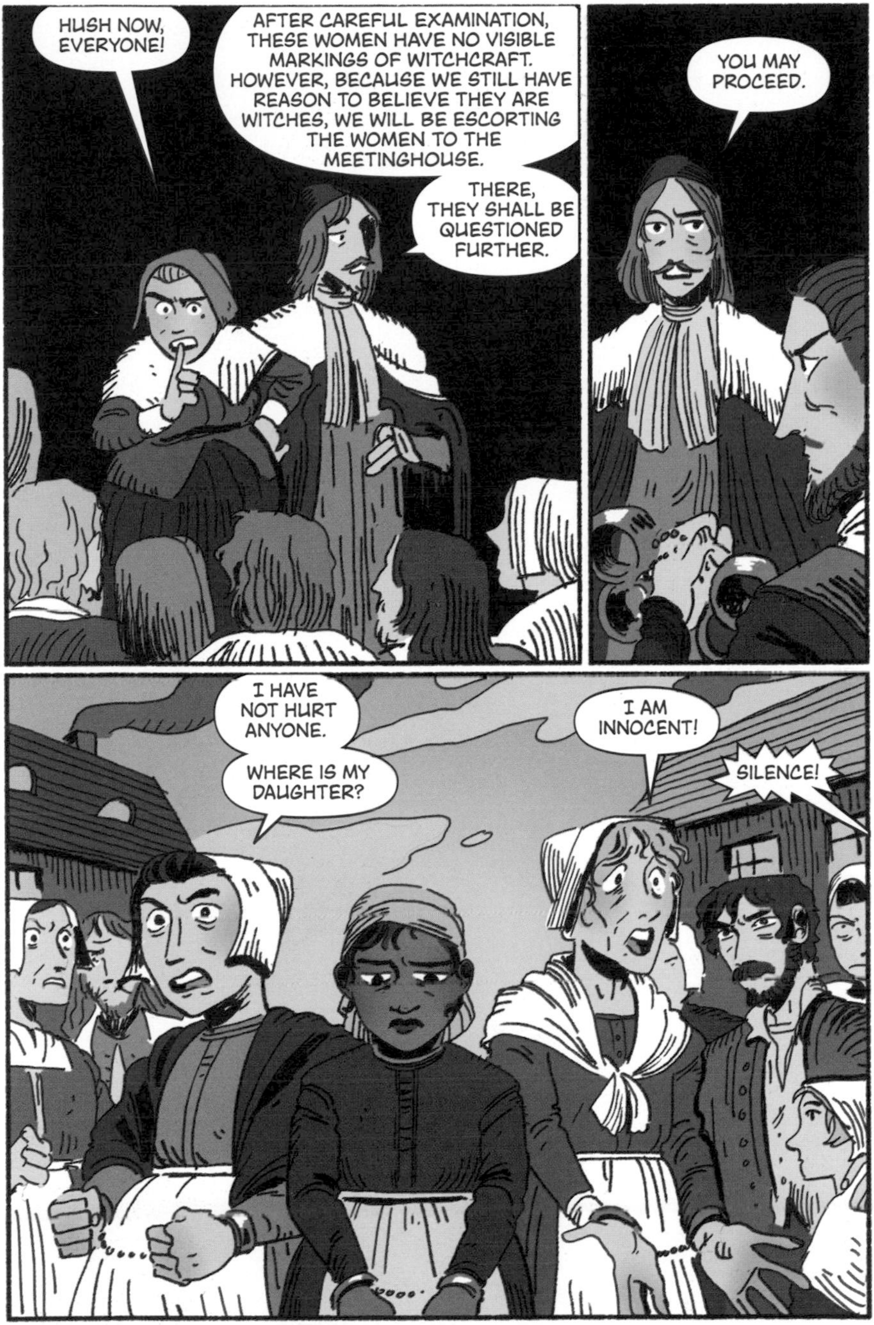
HUSH NOW, EVERYONE!
AFTER CAREFUL EXAMINATION, THESE WOMEN HAVE NO VISIBLE MARKINGS OF WITCHCRAFT. HOWEVER, BECAUSE WE STILL HAVE REASON TO BELIEVE THEY ARE WITCHES, WE WILL BE ESCORTING THE WOMEN TO THE MEETINGHOUSE.
THERE, THEY SHALL BE QUESTIONED FURTHER.
YOU MAY PROCEED.
I HAVE NOT HURT ANYONE.
WHERE IS MY DAUGHTER?
I AM INNOCENT!
SILENCE!

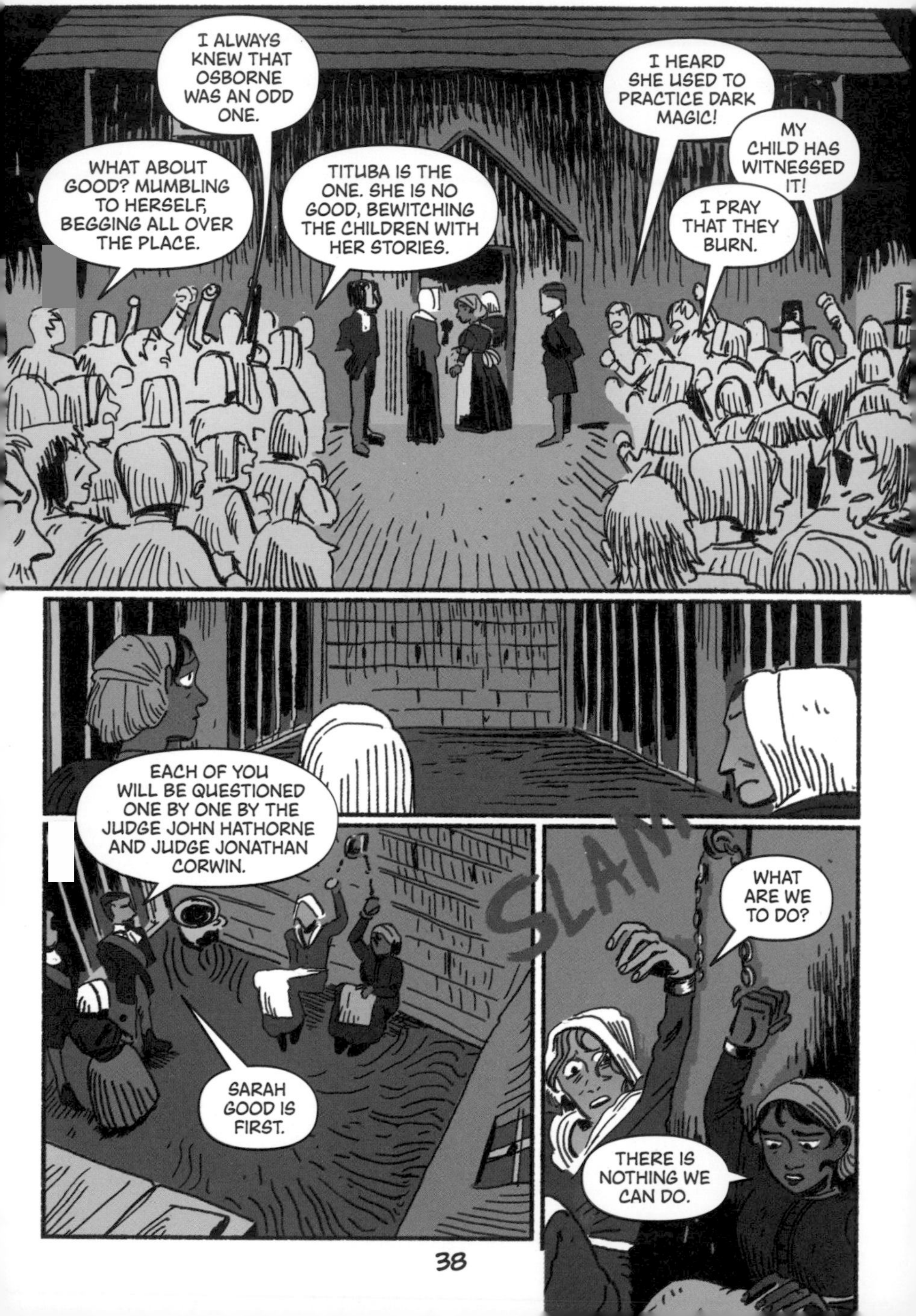
I ALWAYS KNEW THAT OSBORNE WAS AN ODD ONE.
WHAT ABOUT GOOD? MUMBLING TO HERSELF, BEGGING ALL OVER THE PLACE.
TITUBA IS THE ONE. SHE IS NO GOOD, BEWITCHING THE CHILDREN WITH HER STORIES.
I HEARD SHE USED TO PRACTICE DARK MAGIC!
MY CHILD HAS WITNESSED IT!
I PRAY THAT THEY BURN.
EACH OF YOU WILL BE QUESTIONED ONE BY ONE BY THE JUDGE JOHN HATHORNE AND JUDGE JONATHAN CORWIN.
SARAH GOOD IS FIRST.
SLAM
WHAT ARE WE TO DO?
THERE IS NOTHING WE CAN DO.

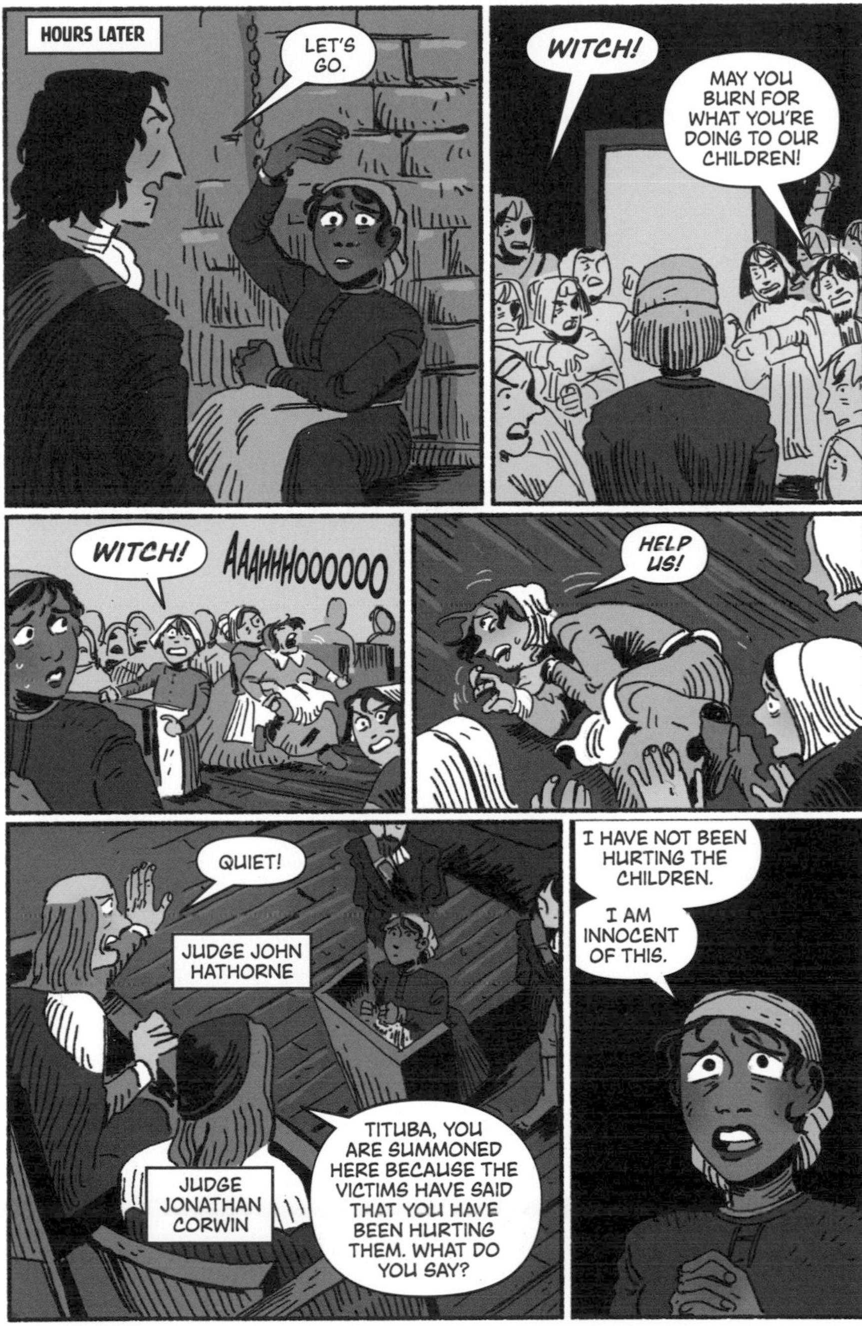
HOURS LATER
LET'S GO.
WITCH!
MAY YOU BURN FOR WHAT YOU'RE DOING TO OUR CHILDREN!
WITCH!
AAAHHHOOOOOO
HELP US!
QUIET!
JUDGE JOHN HATHORNE
JUDGE JONATHAN CORWIN
TITUBA, YOU ARE SUMMONED HERE BECAUSE THE VICTIMS HAVE SAID THAT YOU HAVE BEEN HURTING THEM. WHAT DO YOU SAY?
I HAVE NOT BEEN HURTING THE CHILDREN.
I AM INNOCENT OF THIS.

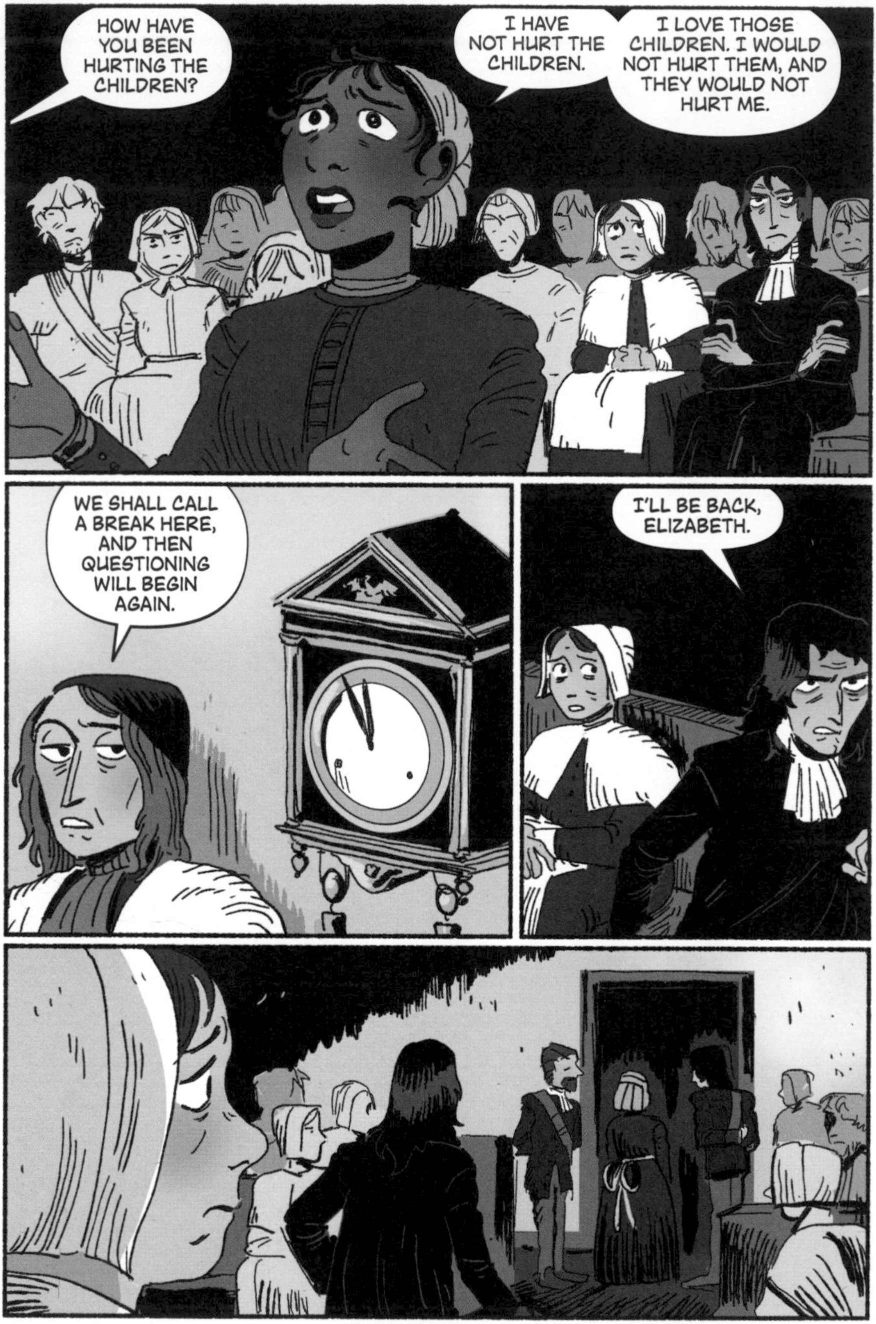
HOW HAVE YOU BEEN HURTING THE CHILDREN?
I HAVE NOT HURT THE CHILDREN.
I LOVE THOSE CHILDREN. I WOULD NOT HURT THEM, AND THEY WOULD NOT HURT ME.
WE SHALL CALL A BREAK HERE, AND THEN QUESTIONING WILL BEGIN AGAIN.
I'LL BE BACK, ELIZABETH.

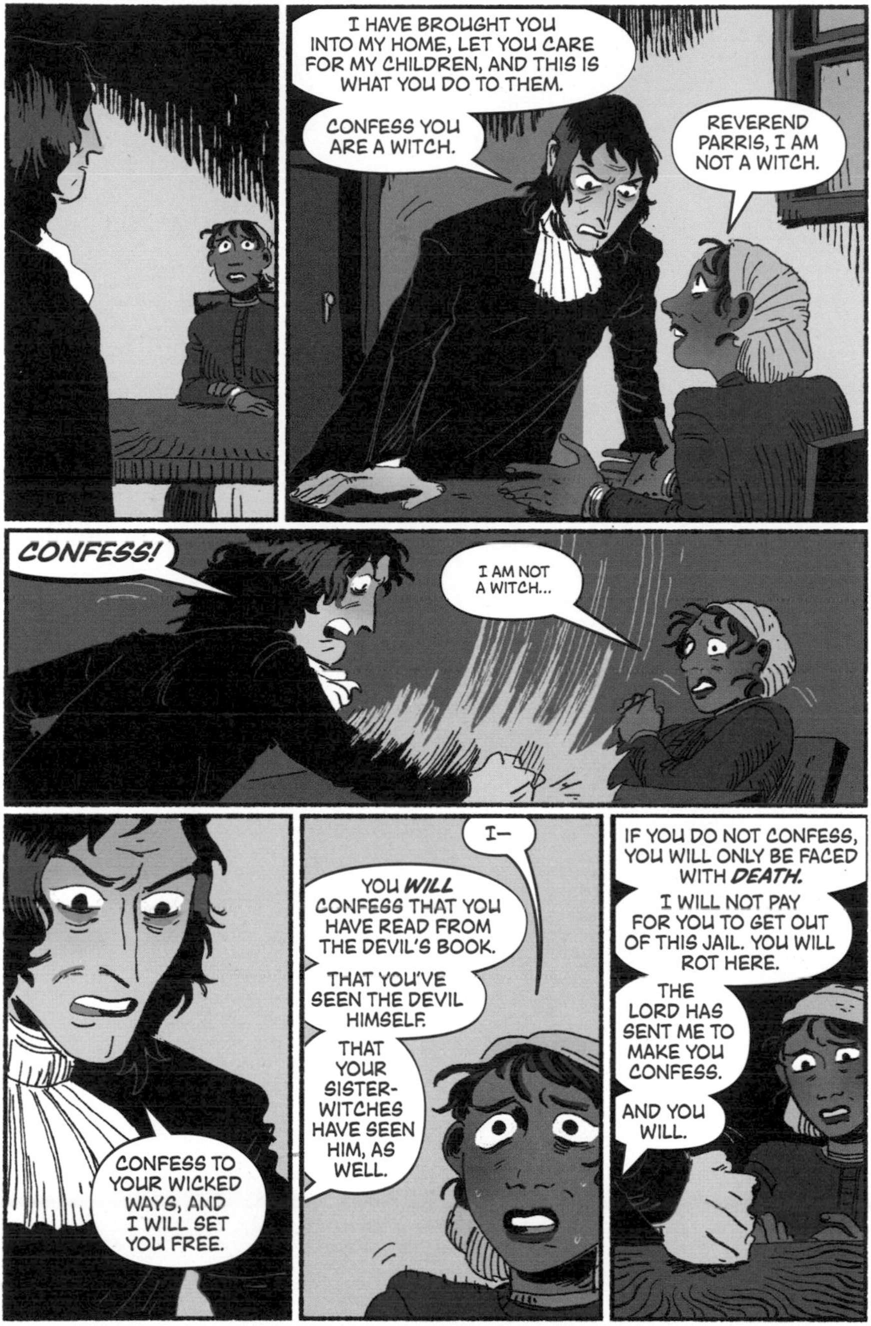
I HAVE BROUGHT YOU INTO MY HOME, LET YOU CARE FOR MY CHILDREN, AND THIS IS WHAT YOU DO TO THEM.
CONFESS YOU ARE A WITCH.
REVEREND PARRIS, I AM NOT A WITCH.
CONFESS!
I AM NOT A WITCH...
CONFESS TO YOUR WICKED WAYS, AND I WILL SET YOU FREE.
I—
YOU WILL CONFESS THAT YOU HAVE READ FROM THE DEVIL'S BOOK.
THAT YOU'VE SEEN THE DEVIL HIMSELF.
THAT YOUR SISTER-WITCHES HAVE SEEN HIM, AS WELL.
IF YOU DO NOT CONFESS, YOU WILL ONLY BE FACED WITH DEATH.
I WILL NOT PAY FOR YOU TO GET OUT OF THIS JAIL. YOU WILL ROT HERE.
THE LORD HAS SENT ME TO MAKE YOU CONFESS.
AND YOU WILL.

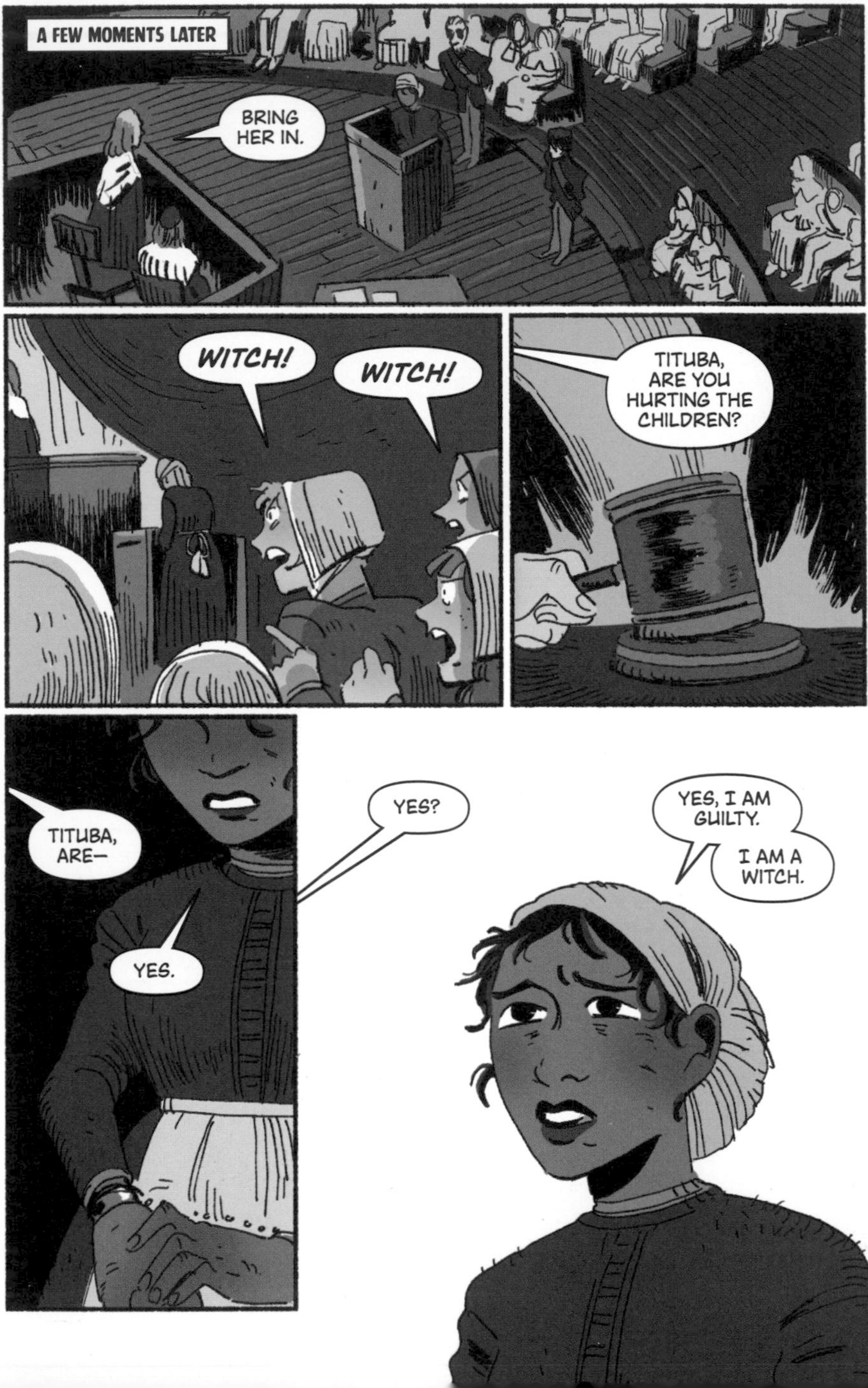
A FEW MOMENTS LATER
BRING HER IN.
WITCH!
WITCH!
TITUBA, ARE YOU HURTING THE CHILDREN?
TITUBA, ARE—
YES.
YES?
YES, I AM GUILTY.
I AM A WITCH.

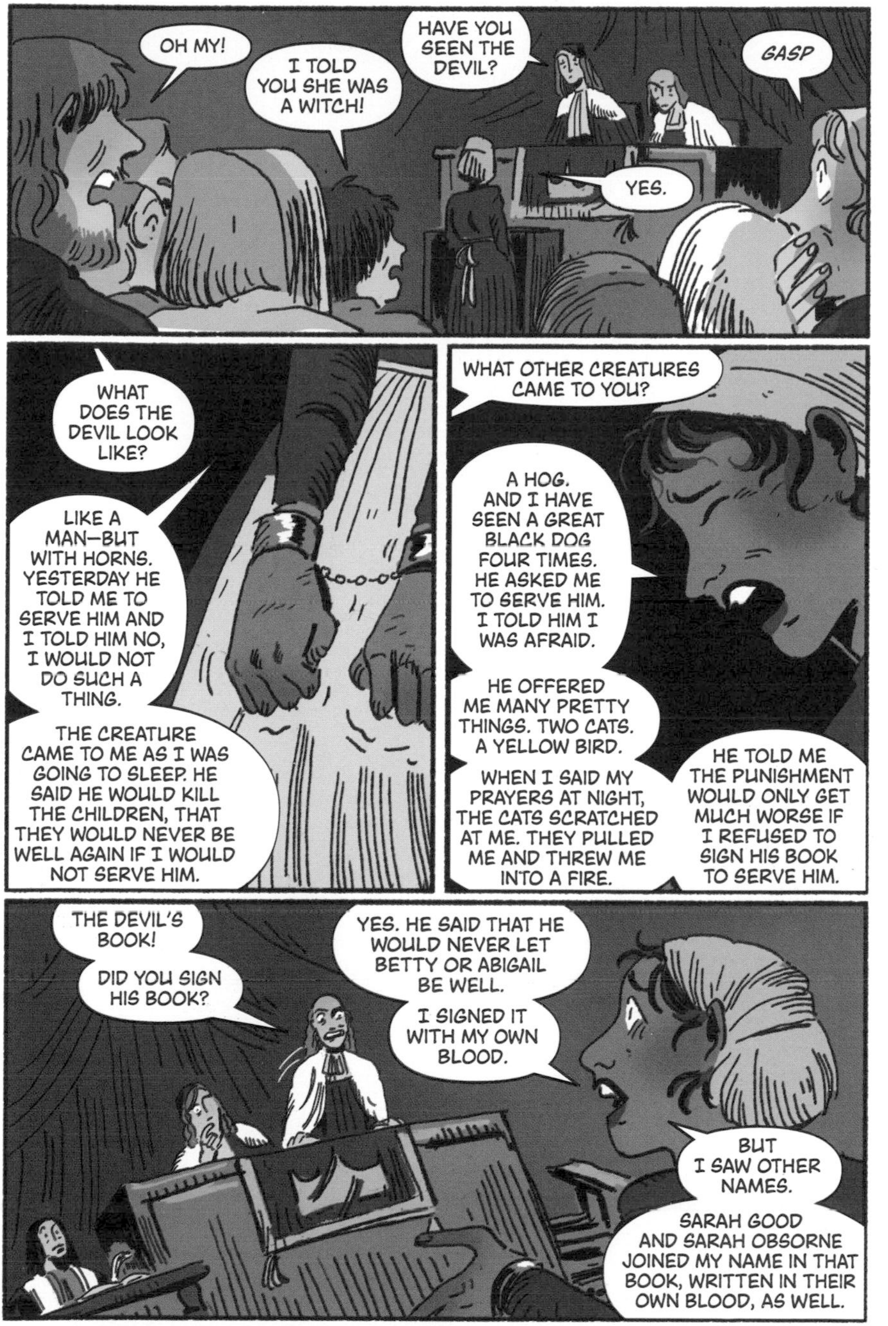
OH MY!
I TOLD YOU SHE WAS A WITCH!
HAVE YOU SEEN THE DEVIL?
GASP
YES.
WHAT DOES THE DEVIL LOOK LIKE?
LIKE A MAN—BUT WITH HORNS. YESTERDAY HE TOLD ME TO SERVE HIM AND I TOLD HIM NO, I WOULD NOT DO SUCH A THING.
THE CREATURE CAME TO ME AS I WAS GOING TO SLEEP. HE SAID HE WOULD KILL THE CHILDREN, THAT THEY WOULD NEVER BE WELL AGAIN IF I WOULD NOT SERVE HIM.
WHAT OTHER CREATURES CAME TO YOU?
A HOG. AND I HAVE SEEN A GREAT BLACK DOG FOUR TIMES. HE ASKED ME TO SERVE HIM. I TOLD HIM I WAS AFRAID.
HE OFFERED ME MANY PRETTY THINGS. TWO CATS. A YELLOW BIRD.
WHEN I SAID MY PRAYERS AT NIGHT, THE CATS SCRATCHED AT ME. THEY PULLED ME AND THREW ME INTO A FIRE.
HE TOLD ME THE PUNISHMENT WOULD ONLY GET MUCH WORSE IF I REFUSED TO SIGN HIS BOOK TO SERVE HIM.
THE DEVIL'S BOOK!
DID YOU SIGN HIS BOOK?
YES. HE SAID THAT HE WOULD NEVER LET BETTY OR ABIGAIL BE WELL.
I SIGNED IT WITH MY OWN BLOOD.
BUT I SAW OTHER NAMES.
SARAH GOOD AND SARAH OBSORNE JOINED MY NAME IN THAT BOOK, WRITTEN IN THEIR OWN BLOOD, AS WELL.

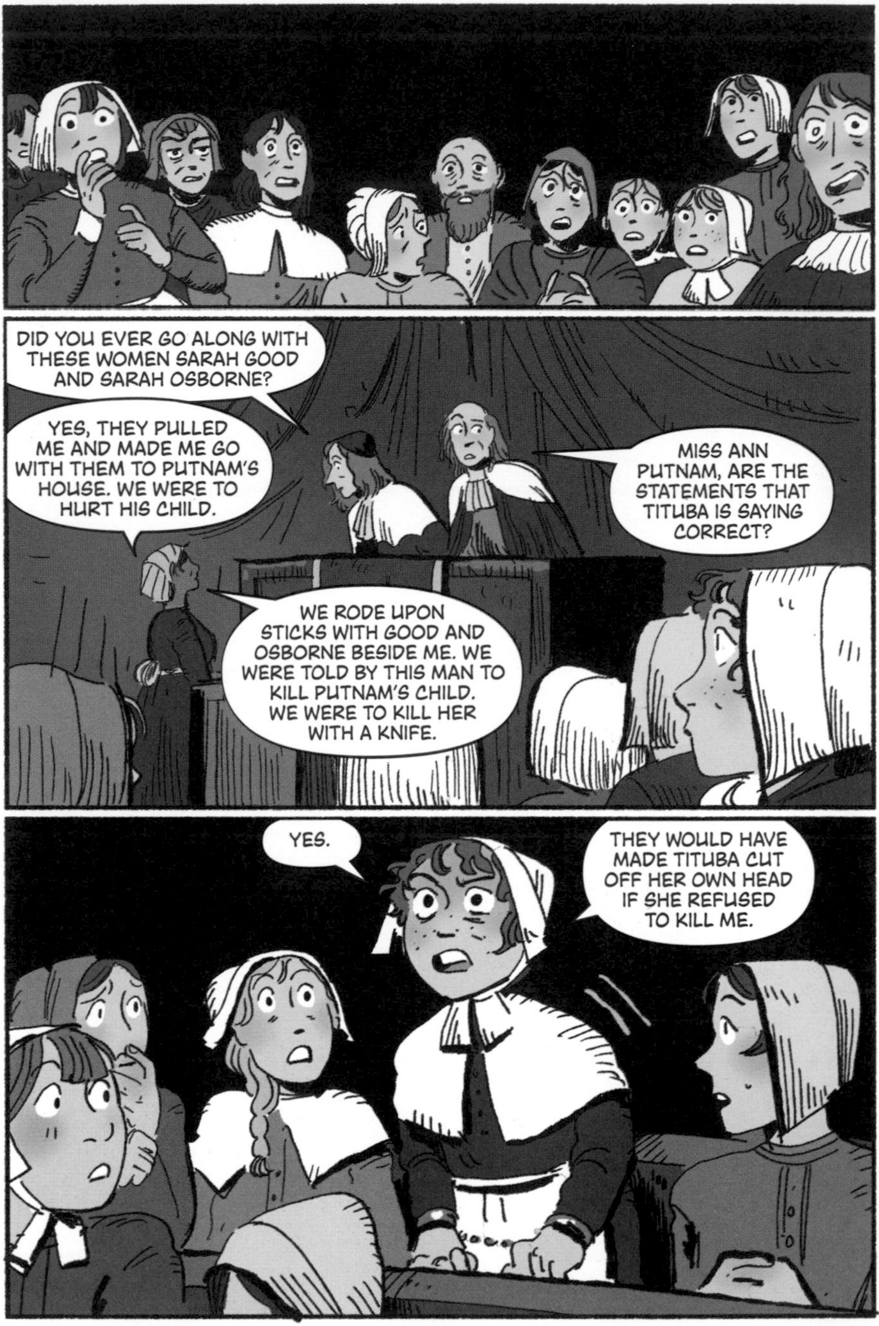
DID YOU EVER GO ALONG WITH THESE WOMEN SARAH GOOD AND SARAH OSBORNE?
YES, THEY PULLED ME AND MADE ME GO WITH THEM TO PUTNAM'S HOUSE. WE WERE TO HURT HIS CHILD.
MISS ANN PUTNAM, ARE THE STATEMENTS THAT TITUBA IS SAYING CORRECT?
WE RODE UPON STICKS WITH GOOD AND OSBORNE BESIDE ME. WE WERE TOLD BY THIS MAN TO KILL PUTNAM'S CHILD. WE WERE TO KILL HER WITH A KNIFE.
YES.
THEY WOULD HAVE MADE TITUBA CUT OFF HER OWN HEAD IF SHE REFUSED TO KILL ME.

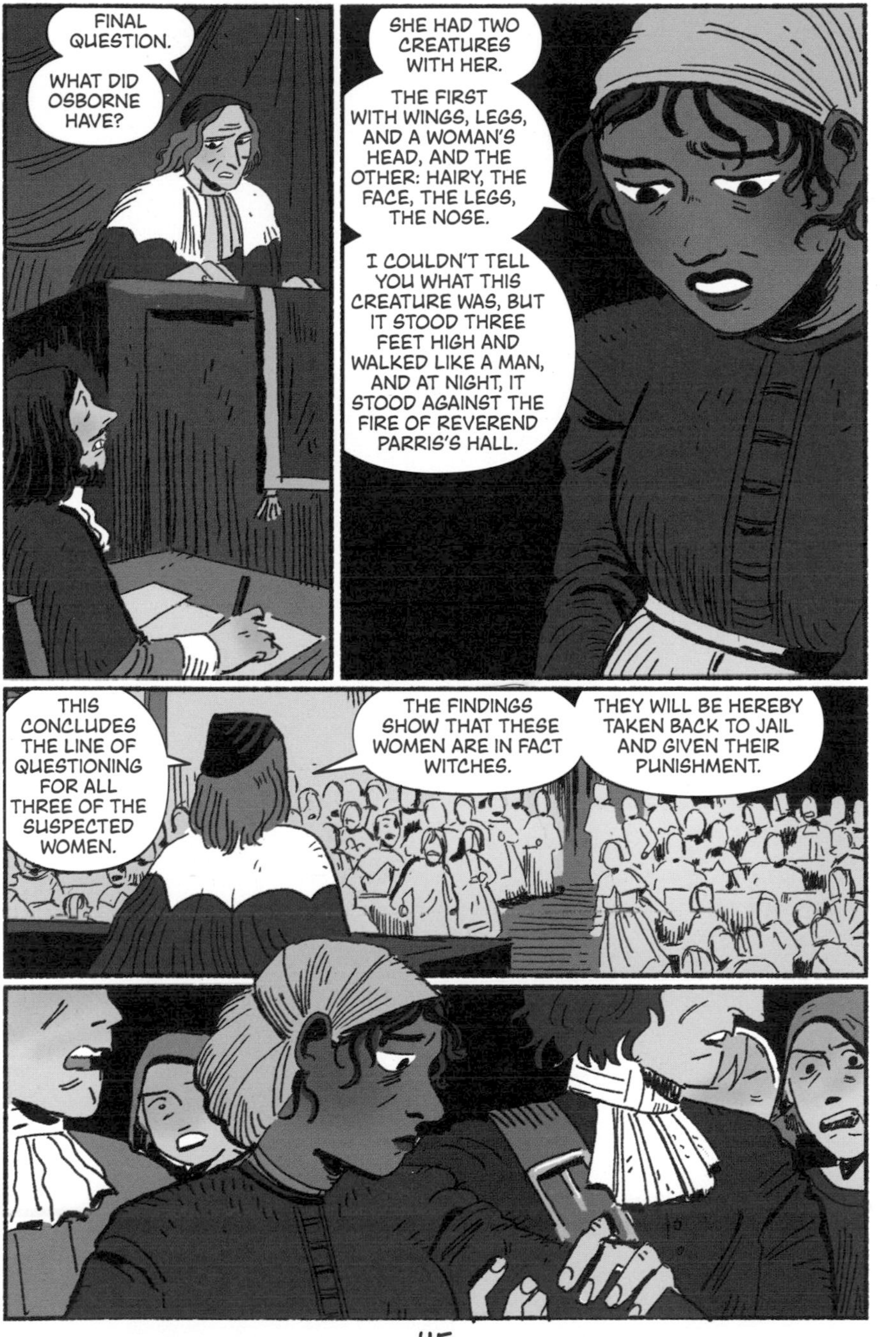
FINAL QUESTION.
WHAT DID OSBORNE HAVE?
SHE HAD TWO CREATURES WITH HER.
THE FIRST WITH WINGS, LEGS, AND A WOMAN'S HEAD, AND THE OTHER: HAIRY, THE FACE, THE LEGS, THE NOSE.
I COULDN'T TELL YOU WHAT THIS CREATURE WAS, BUT IT STOOD THREE FEET HIGH AND WALKED LIKE A MAN, AND AT NIGHT, IT STOOD AGAINST THE FIRE OF REVEREND PARRIS'S HALL.
THIS CONCLUDES THE LINE OF QUESTIONING FOR ALL THREE OF THE SUSPECTED WOMEN.
THE FINDINGS SHOW THAT THESE WOMEN ARE IN FACT WITCHES.
THEY WILL BE HEREBY TAKEN BACK TO JAIL AND GIVEN THEIR PUNISHMENT.

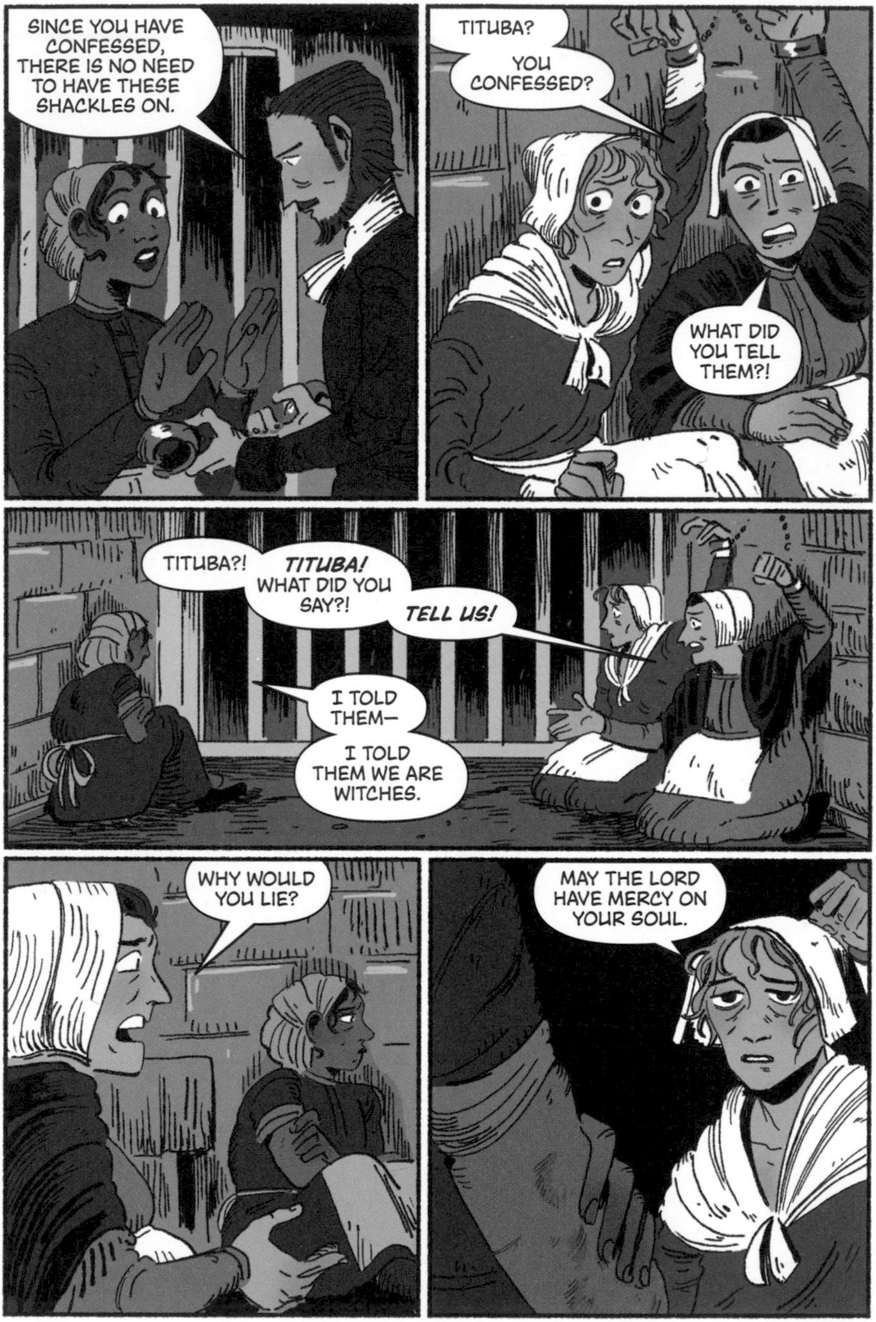
SINCE YOU HAVE CONFESSED, THERE IS NO NEED TO HAVE THESE SHACKLES ON.
TITUBA?
YOU CONFESSED?
WHAT DID YOU TELL THEM?!
TITUBA?!
TITUBA! WHAT DID YOU SAY?!
TELL US!
I TOLD THEM—
I TOLD THEM WE ARE WITCHES.
WHY WOULD YOU LIE?
MAY THE LORD HAVE MERCY ON YOUR SOUL.

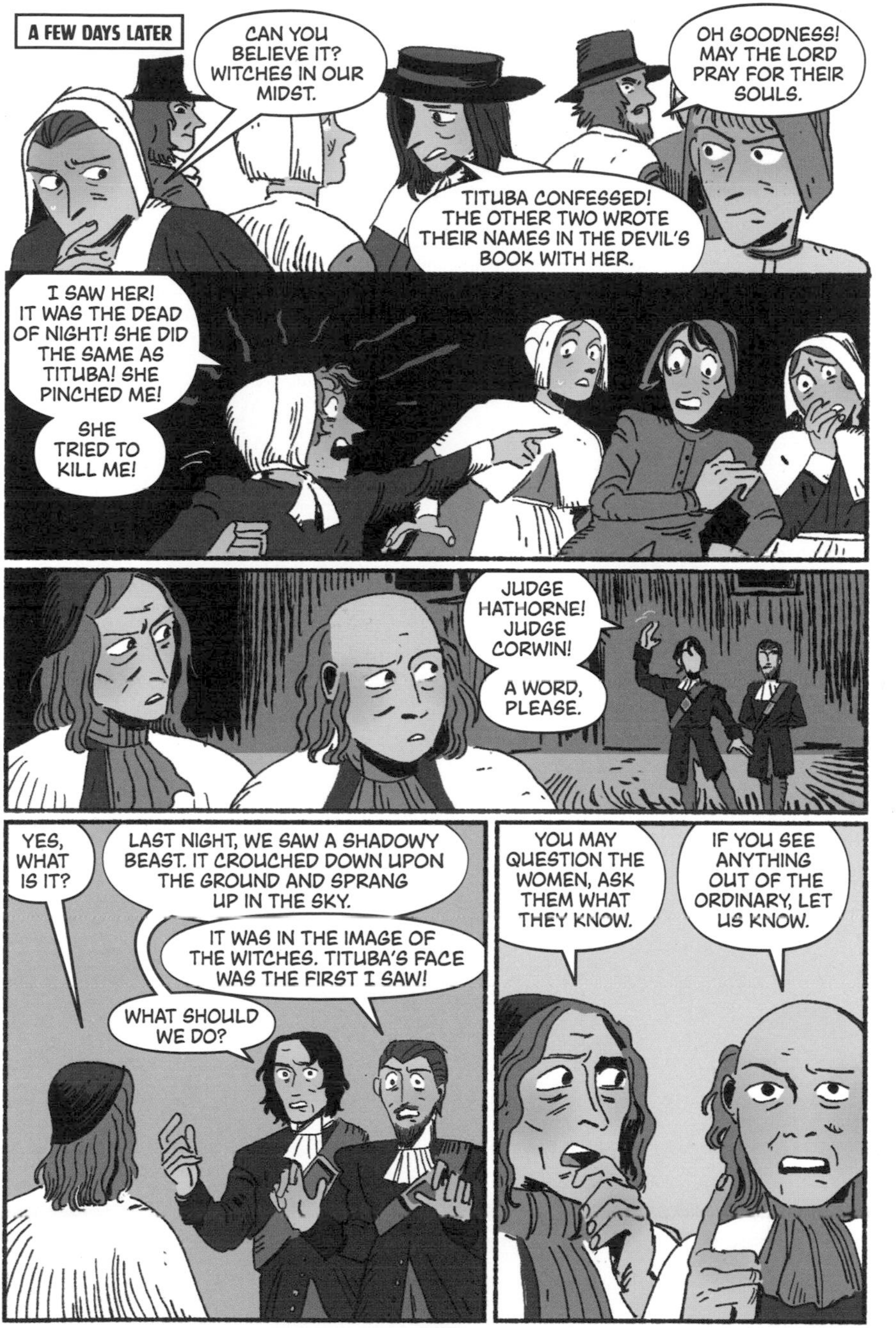
A FEW DAYS LATER
CAN YOU BELIEVE IT? WITCHES IN OUR MIDST.
OH GOODNESS! MAY THE LORD PRAY FOR THEIR SOULS.
TITUBA CONFESSED! THE OTHER TWO WROTE THEIR NAMES IN THE DEVIL'S BOOK WITH HER.
I SAW HER! IT WAS THE DEAD OF NIGHT! SHE DID THE SAME AS TITUBA! SHE PINCHED ME!
SHE TRIED TO KILL ME!
JUDGE HATHORNE! JUDGE CORWIN!
A WORD, PLEASE.
YES, WHAT IS IT?
LAST NIGHT, WE SAW A SHADOWY BEAST. IT CROUCHED DOWN UPON THE GROUND AND SPRANG UP IN THE SKY.
IT WAS IN THE IMAGE OF THE WITCHES. TITUBA'S FACE WAS THE FIRST I SAW!
WHAT SHOULD WE DO?
YOU MAY QUESTION THE WOMEN, ASK THEM WHAT THEY KNOW.
IF YOU SEE ANYTHING OUT OF THE ORDINARY, LET US KNOW.

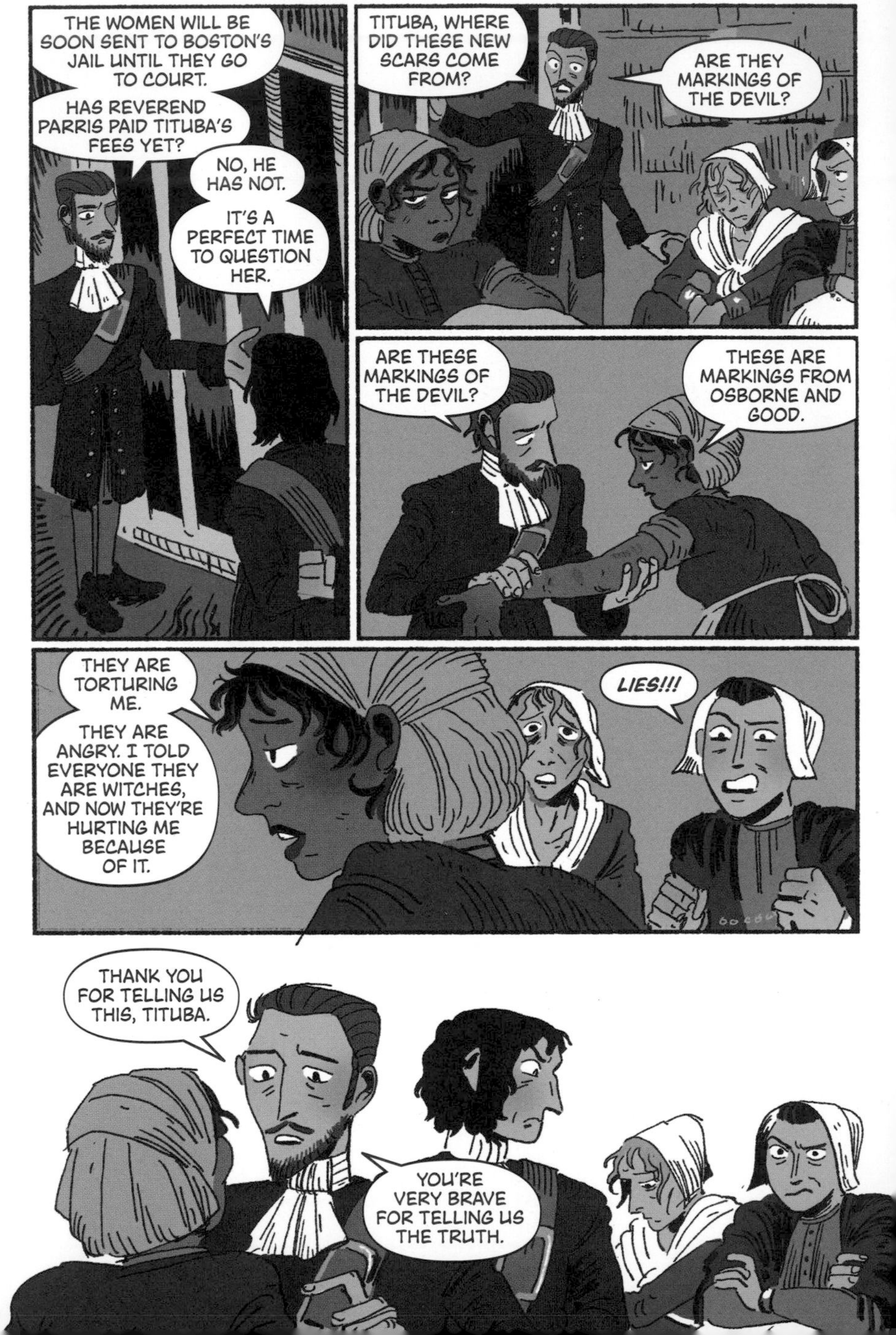
THE WOMEN WILL BE SOON SENT TO BOSTON'S JAIL UNTIL THEY GO TO COURT.
HAS REVEREND PARRIS PAID TITUBA'S FEES YET?
NO, HE HAS NOT.
IT'S A PERFECT TIME TO QUESTION HER.
TITUBA, WHERE DID THESE NEW SCARS COME FROM?
ARE THEY MARKINGS OF THE DEVIL?
ARE THESE MARKINGS OF THE DEVIL?
THESE ARE MARKINGS FROM OSBORNE AND GOOD.
THEY ARE TORTURING ME.
THEY ARE ANGRY. I TOLD EVERYONE THEY ARE WITCHES, AND NOW THEY'RE HURTING ME BECAUSE OF IT.
LIES!!!
THANK YOU FOR TELLING US THIS, TITUBA.
YOU'RE VERY BRAVE FOR TELLING US THE TRUTH.

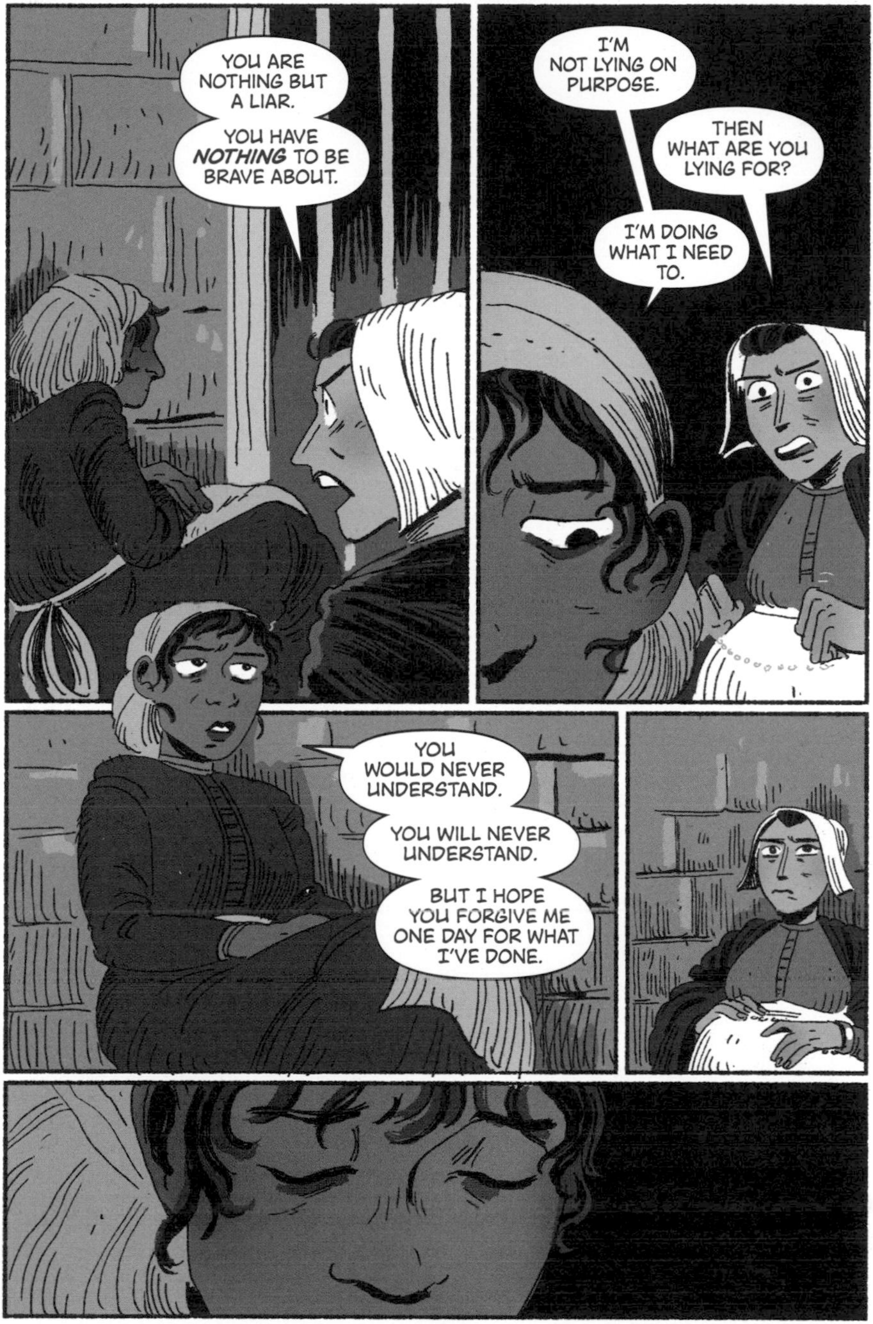
YOU ARE NOTHING BUT A LIAR.
YOU HAVE *NOTHING* TO BE BRAVE ABOUT.
I'M NOT LYING ON PURPOSE.
THEN WHAT ARE YOU LYING FOR?
I'M DOING WHAT I NEED TO.
YOU WOULD NEVER UNDERSTAND.
YOU WILL NEVER UNDERSTAND.
BUT I HOPE YOU FORGIVE ME ONE DAY FOR WHAT I'VE DONE.

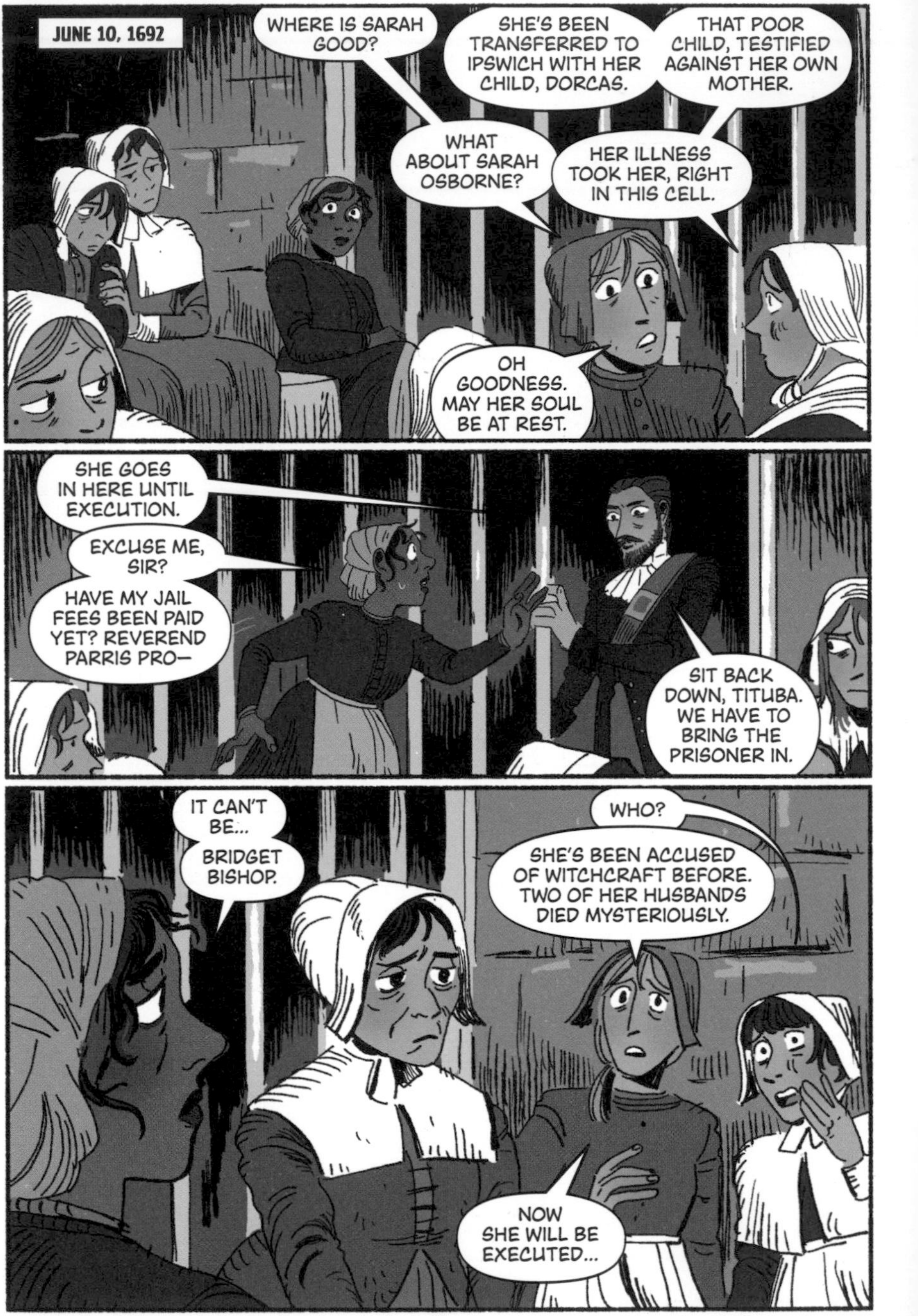

JUNE 10, 1692
WHERE IS SARAH GOOD?
SHE'S BEEN TRANSFERRED TO IPSWICH WITH HER CHILD, DORCAS.
THAT POOR CHILD, TESTIFIED AGAINST HER OWN MOTHER.
WHAT ABOUT SARAH OSBORNE?
HER ILLNESS TOOK HER, RIGHT IN THIS CELL.
OH GOODNESS. MAY HER SOUL BE AT REST.
SHE GOES IN HERE UNTIL EXECUTION.
EXCUSE ME, SIR?
HAVE MY JAIL FEES BEEN PAID YET? REVEREND PARRIS PRO—
SIT BACK DOWN, TITUBA. WE HAVE TO BRING THE PRISONER IN.
IT CAN'T BE...
BRIDGET BISHOP.
WHO?
SHE'S BEEN ACCUSED OF WITCHCRAFT BEFORE. TWO OF HER HUSBANDS DIED MYSTERIOUSLY.
NOW SHE WILL BE EXECUTED...

Bridget Bishop

Bridget Bishop was born in 1630s Norwich, England. Bridget was married three times. Her first marriage was to Samuel Wasselbe, who died around the time she settled in New England. The second was to Thomas Oliver, who was also a widower. Together, they had one child, Christian. Thomas died in 1679, and Bridget inherited his land.

The following year, there were whispers that perhaps Bridget was a witch. She was accused of witchcraft because many thought she had something to do with the deaths of her late husbands, while others contended they saw her specter—a haunting spirit or soul that is a visible ghost—flying over them. Bridget denied all the claims and married her last husband, Edward Bishop, in 1687.

But the accusations of witchcraft didn't stop. Ann Putnam Jr., Mercy Lewis, Mary Walcott, and Elizabeth Hubbard accused Bridget, as well as Mary Warren, of tormenting them. Bridget was arrested on April 19, and was quickly found guilty. Two months later, on June 10, she was led to Gallows Hill where she was hung, making her the first innocent victim to die in Salem by execution.

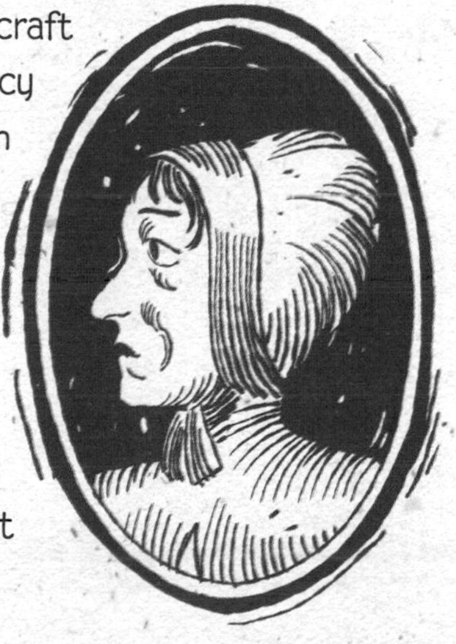

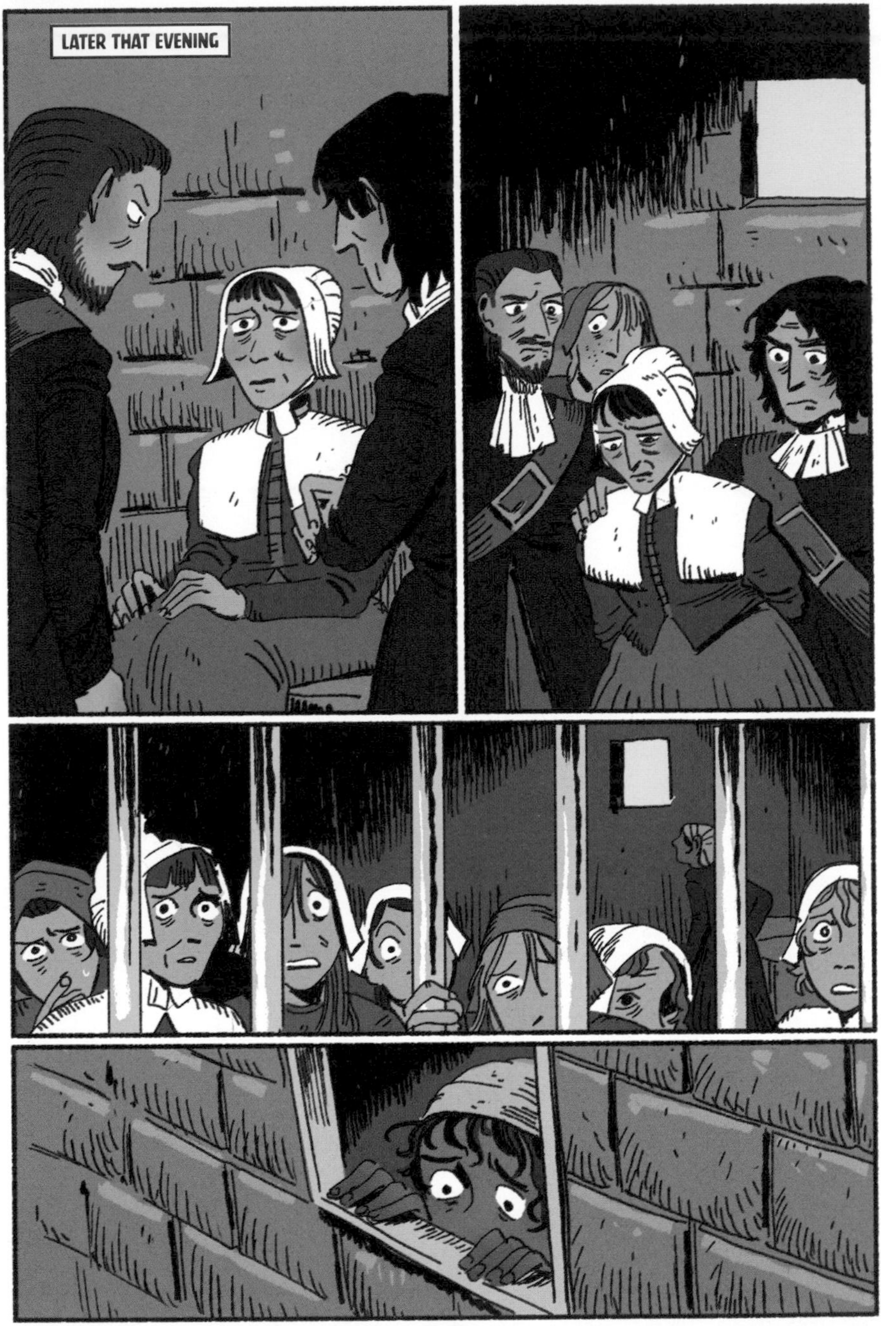
LATER THAT EVENING

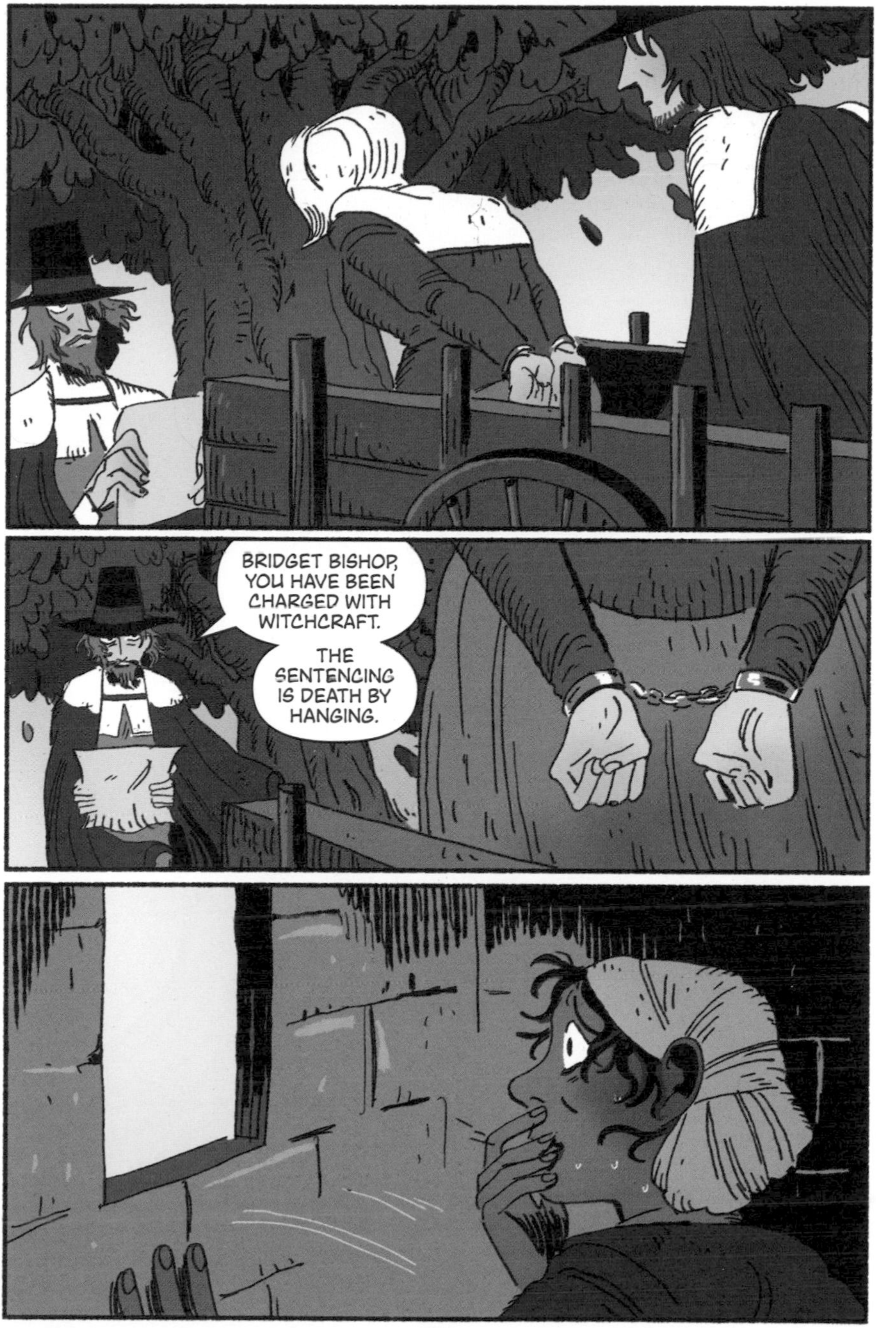
BRIDGET BISHOP, YOU HAVE BEEN CHARGED WITH WITCHCRAFT.
THE SENTENCING IS DEATH BY HANGING.

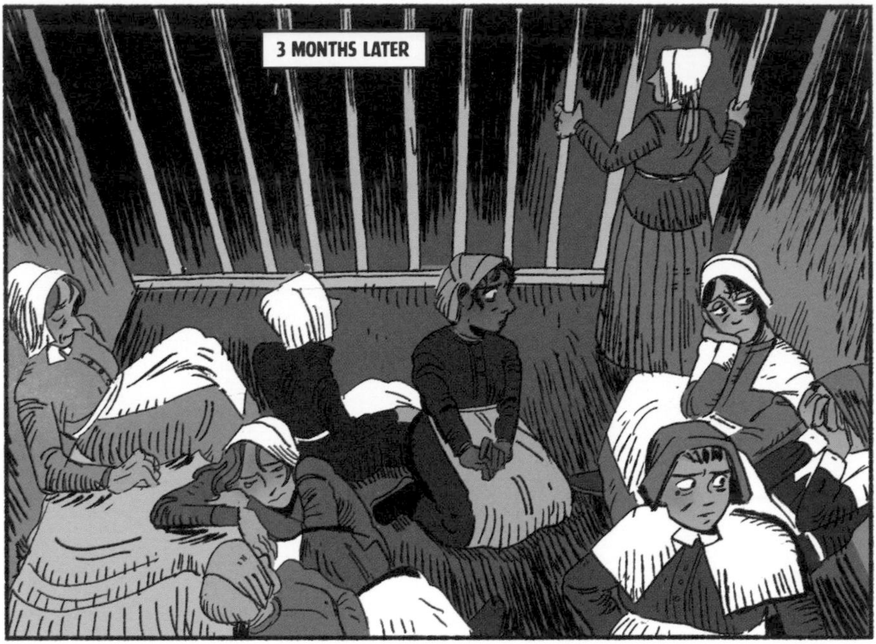
3 MONTHS LATER

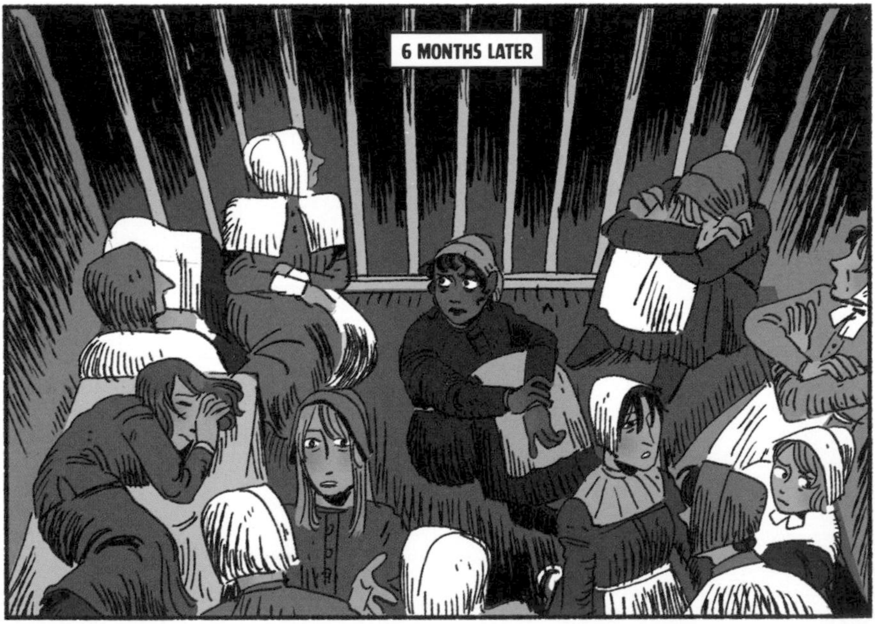
6 MONTHS LATER

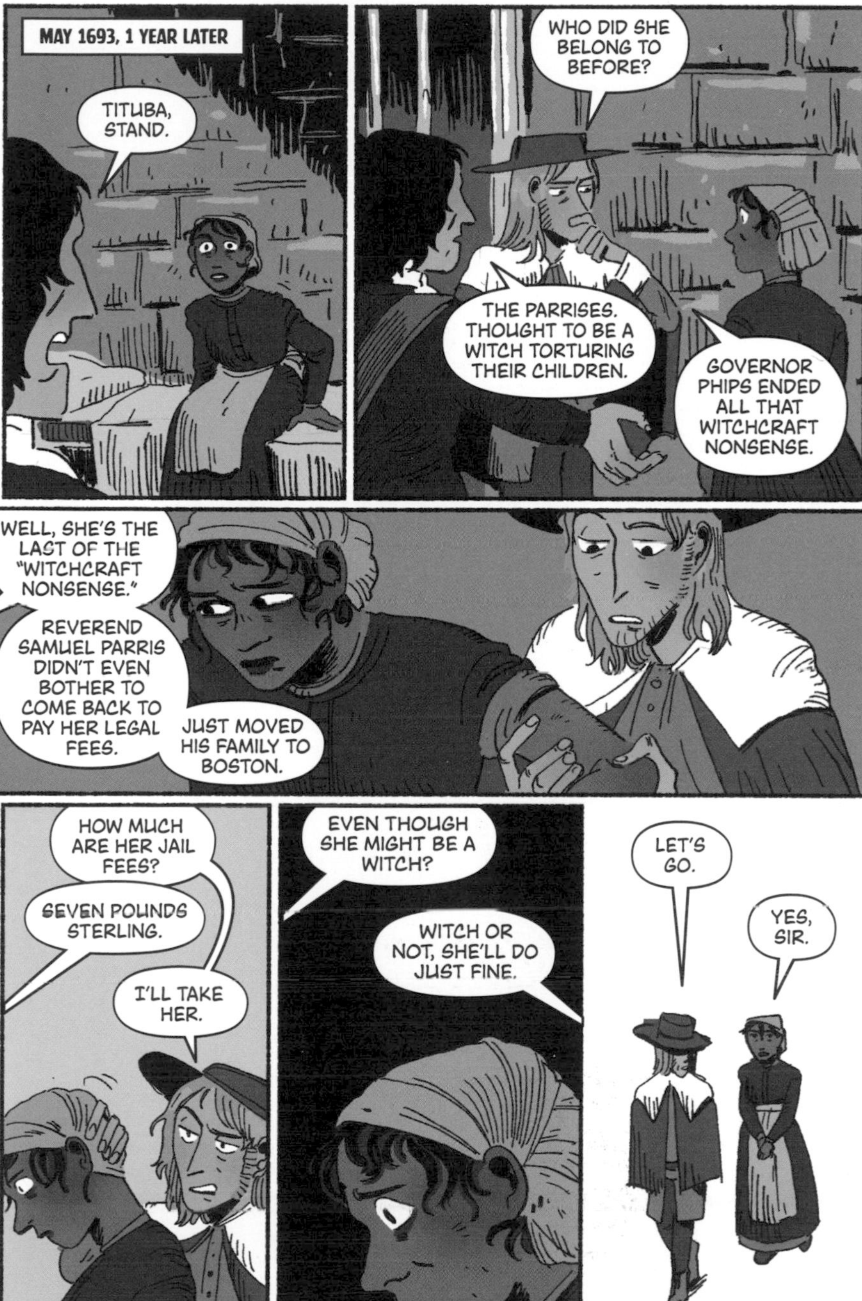
MAY 1693, 1 YEAR LATER
TITUBA, STAND.
WHO DID SHE BELONG TO BEFORE?
THE PARRISES. THOUGHT TO BE A WITCH TORTURING THEIR CHILDREN.
GOVERNOR PHIPS ENDED ALL THAT WITCHCRAFT NONSENSE.
WELL, SHE'S THE LAST OF THE "WITCHCRAFT NONSENSE."
REVEREND SAMUEL PARRIS DIDN'T EVEN BOTHER TO COME BACK TO PAY HER LEGAL FEES.
JUST MOVED HIS FAMILY TO BOSTON.
HOW MUCH ARE HER JAIL FEES?
SEVEN POUNDS STERLING.
I'LL TAKE HER.
EVEN THOUGH SHE MIGHT BE A WITCH?
WITCH OR NOT, SHE'LL DO JUST FINE.
LET'S GO.
YES, SIR.

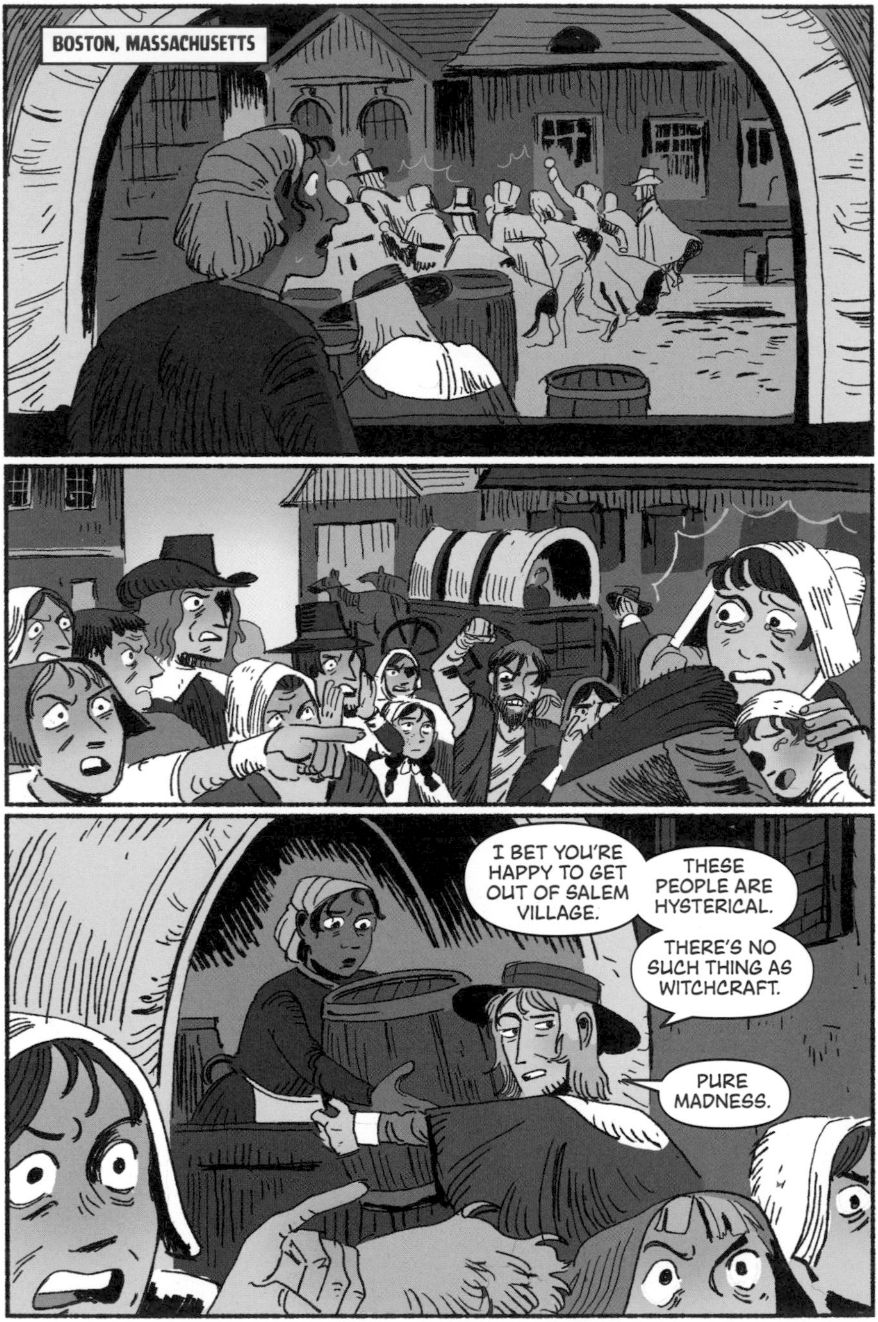
BOSTON, MASSACHUSETTS
I BET YOU'RE HAPPY TO GET OUT OF SALEM VILLAGE.
THESE PEOPLE ARE HYSTERICAL.
THERE'S NO SUCH THING AS WITCHCRAFT.
PURE MADNESS.

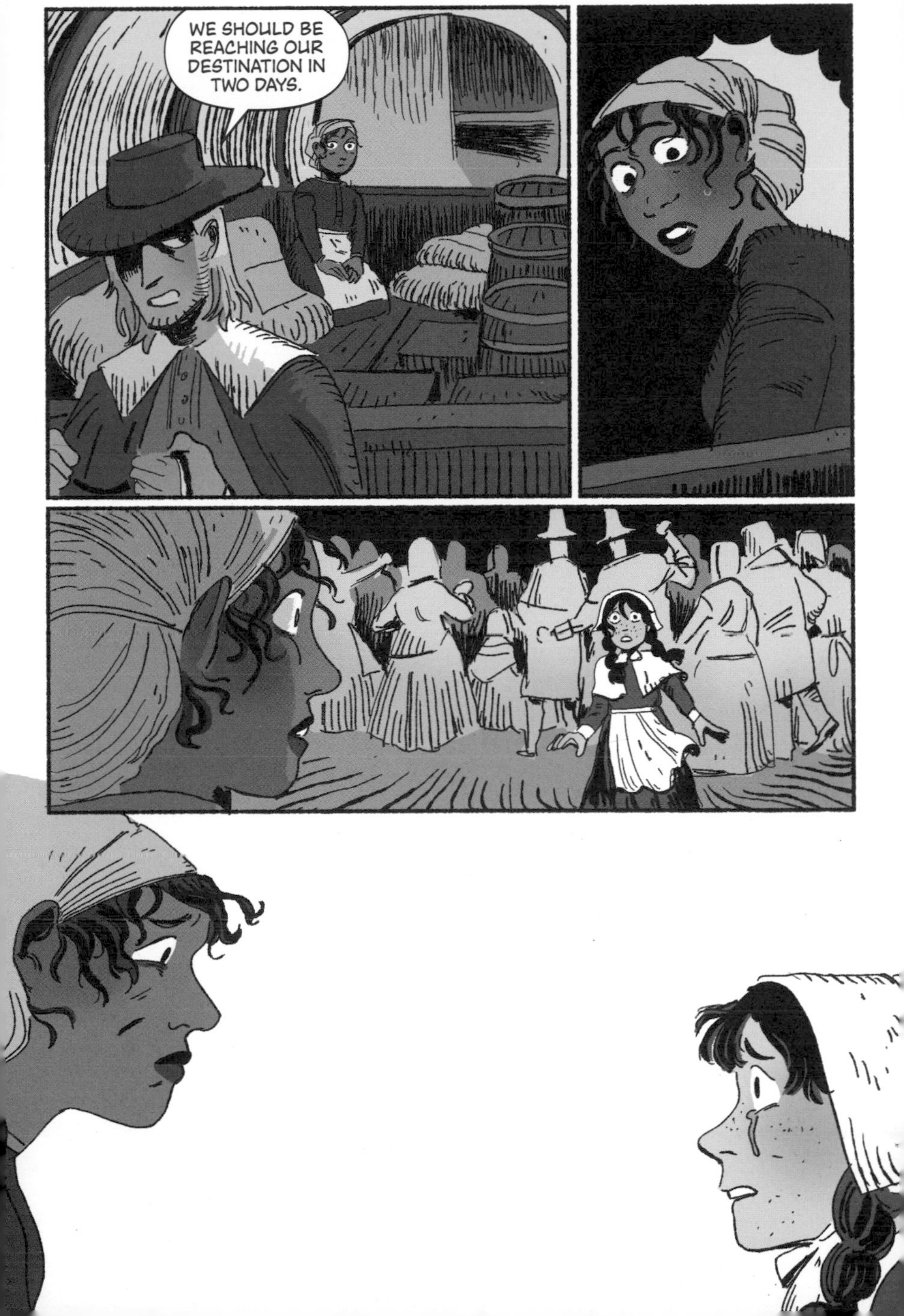
WE SHOULD BE REACHING OUR DESTINATION IN TWO DAYS.

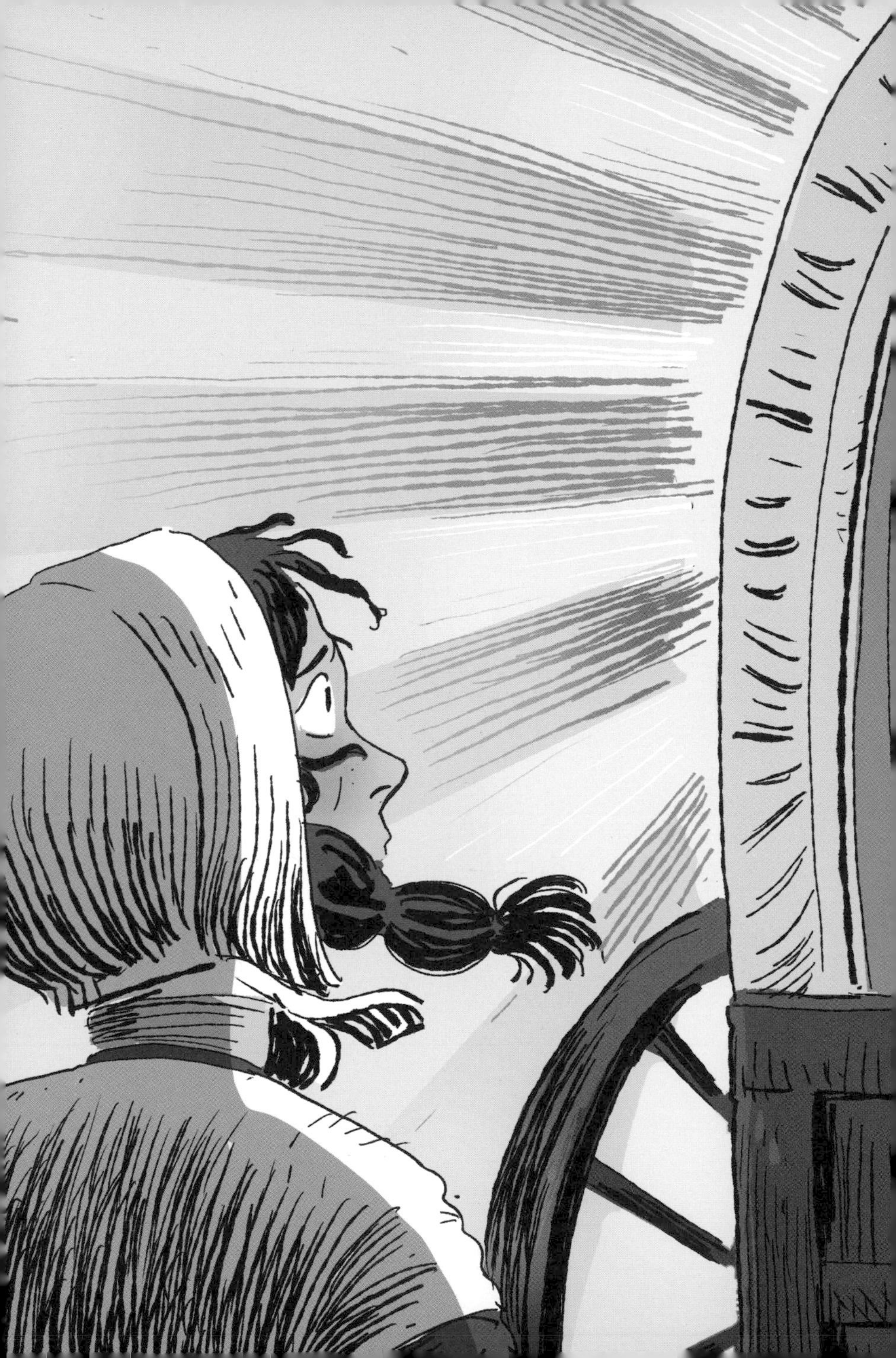

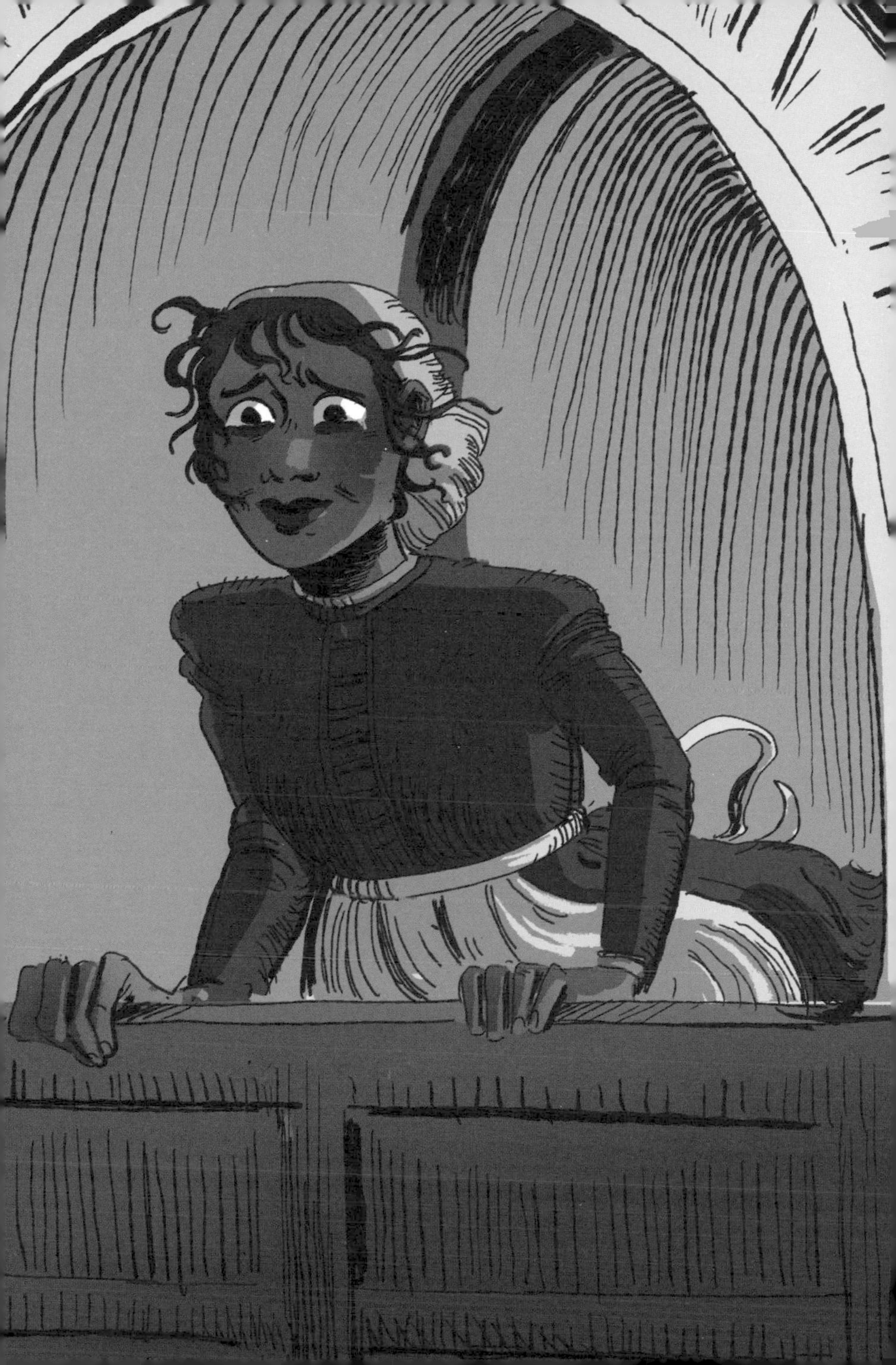

Conclusion

After she was taken away from Salem Village, Tituba's fate is unknown to history. Tituba's "confession" spared her the fate of death and further punishment from Reverend Parris. It's thought that Tituba wasn't trying to persecute anyone—she was just trying to survive.

The fate of John Indian is unknown. Sources are unclear if he was sold with Tituba or separately from her. Tituba's daughter, Violet, reportedly stayed with the Parrises until she was an adult, but not much is known of her after that. After Tituba's confession, the accusations of witchcraft spread throughout Massachusetts. Villagers, neighbors, friends, and family kept accusing each other of witchcraft. The afflicted girls would go on to accuse many others, including Rebecca Nurse, Elizabeth Howe, and seventeen others who were executed by hanging. Sarah Good was moved from the prison to Ipswich, Massachusetts, and executed by hanging. Sarah Osborne and four others died in jail. On October 29, 1692, the Salem witch trials court officially closed. In May 1693, everyone who was held in prison on suspicion of witchcraft was finally freed.

Although the trials ended, there's still speculation on why they happened in the first place. Some think that perhaps the afflicted girls were bored and wanted to have fun. Others think that the girls may have been poisoned by ergot, a poisonous fungus found when rye goes bad. However, many think that this was a case of mass hysteria—a condition where a large group of people suddenly begins to exhibit strange and sometimes extreme behavior.

Mass hysteria has also contributed to other "witch hunts" all over the world, one of the most famous being the modern witch hunt of the McCarthy era. In the 1950s, US senator Joseph McCarthy claimed that communist spies had infiltrated the US government, and he accused many innocent Americans of treason, playing on people's fears in order to turn friends, loved ones, and neighbors against one another. In 1953, the American playwright Arthur Miller wrote *The Crucible*, a play about the Salem witch trials which reflects the McCarthy-era witch hunts.

In 2001, Massachusetts formally announced that those who had been convicted, tried, and killed during the Salem witch trials were innocent. Today, Salem Village is different. It is now Danvers, Massachusetts. In Salem Town (now Salem, Massachusetts), you can visit local shops, witchy spots, and museums telling the stories of the women and men accused of witchcraft, often for no other reason than being different.

Timeline of the Salem Witch Trials

1689 — Reverend Samuel Parris moves with his family to Salem Village and becomes the church minister

1692 — In January, Betty Parris and Abigail Williams start to have fits that cause them to thrash about and scream

— On February 24, Dr. William Griggs deems nothing physically wrong with the children, but says they're "bewitched"

— On February 26, Betty and Abigail have fits again and accuse Tituba of witchcraft

— After being arrested, Tituba confesses to witchcraft on March 1

— On May 27, the Salem witch trials court is formed

— From June to September, Bridget Bishop is the first accused to be hanged for witchcraft, followed by Sarah Good, Elizabeth Howe, Rebecca Nurse, Sarah Wildes, Susannah Martin, John Proctor, Martha Carrier, George Jacobs, George Burroughs, John Willard, Mary Easty, Alice Parker, Ann Pudeator, Martha Corey, Mary Parker, Wilmot Redd, Margaret Scott, and Samuel Wardwell

1693 — In May, Tituba is released from jail to a new enslaver

— Everyone who is still in jail for witchcraft is freed; the witch trials officially end

2001 — The state of Massachusetts finally names and declares innocent all victims of the Salem witch trials

Bibliography

*Books for young readers

Goss, K. David. *Daily Life During the Salem Witch Trials*.
Santa Barbara, CA: Greenwood, 2012.

Goss, K. David. *The Salem Witch Trials: A Reference Guide*.
Westport, CT: Greenwood Press, 2008.

*Holub, Joan. *What Were the Salem Witch Trials?* New York:
Penguin Workshop, 2015.

*MacBain, Jenny. *Primary Sources in American History: The Salem
Witch Trials*. New York: Rosen Publishing Group, Inc, 2003.

*Reynolds, Donna. *Turning Points: The Salem Witch Trials*. New York:
Cavendish Square, 2021.

*Schanzer, Rosalyn. *Witches! The Absolutely True Tale of Disaster in
Salem*. Washington, DC: National Geographic Society, 2011.

Starkey, Marion L. *The Devil in Massachusetts*. New York:
Alfred A. Knopf, 1949.

ABOUT THE CREATORS

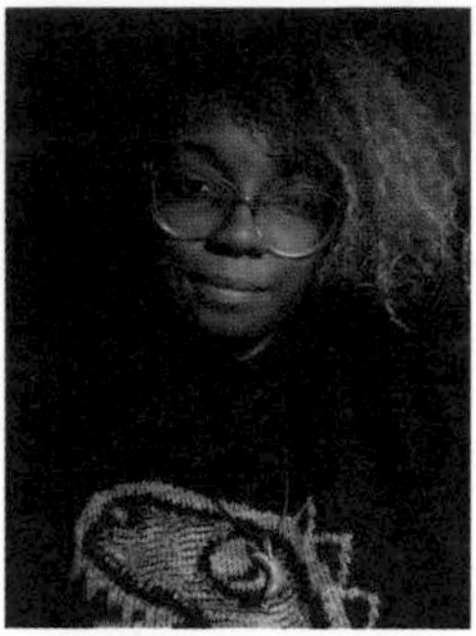

Insha Fitzpatrick is an author of books and graphic novels, including *Who Sparked the Montgomery Bus Boycott? Rosa Parks*, *Hanging with Vampires* from Quirk Books, and the coauthor of the series *Oh My Gods!* She founded DIS/MEMBER, a genre website dedicated to all things horror, and when she's not writing, she's catching up on horror films or consumed by reality TV.

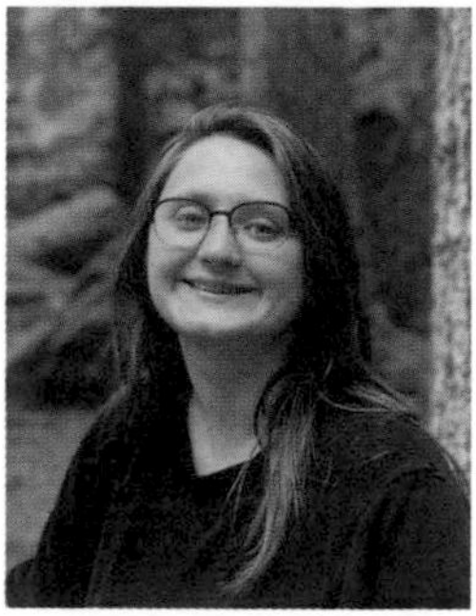

Rowan MacColl is a comic artist and illustrator from New England who loves historical clothing, ghost stories, and, of course, cats. She is constantly mixing up her coffee cup and her ink cup while juggling way too many personal projects, but she hasn't poisoned herself yet. Rowan wants to draw and write stories about what makes people human. Some of her recent work includes the art of the graphic novel *Nightmare in Savannah* and her personal online comic *Kingfisher*. You can find more of her work at www.rowanmaccoll.com.